ENCOUNTERS

ENCOUNTERS
Conversations on Life and Writing

HÉLÈNE CIXOUS AND FRÉDÉRIC-YVES JEANNET

TRANSLATED BY
BEVERLEY BIE BRAHIC

polity

First published in French as *Rencontre Terrestre* © Éditions Galilée, 2005.

This English edition © Polity Press, 2013

Polity Press
65 Bridge Street
Cambridge CB2 1UR, UK

Polity Press
350 Main Street
Malden, MA 02148, USA

ISBN-13: 978-0-7456-5386-0
ISBN-13: 978-0-7456-5387-7(pb)

A catalogue record for this book is available from the British Library.

Typeset in 10.75 on 14 pt Janson Text
by Servis Filmsetting Ltd, Stockport, Cheshire
Printed and bound in Great Britain by MPG Books Group Limited,
Bodmin, Cornwall

The publisher has used its best endeavours to ensure that the URLs for external websites referred to in this book are correct and active at the time of going to press. However, the publisher has no responsibility for the websites and can make no guarantee that a site will remain live or that the content is or will remain appropriate.

Every effort has been made to trace all copyright holders, but if any have been inadvertently overlooked the publisher will be pleased to include any necessary credits in any subsequent reprint or edition.

For further information on Polity, visit our website: www.politybooks.com

CONTENTS

At first, everything was recorded at a table in Paris. Then oceans intervened. Change of scene: the interview continued in writing. Which made for a different style naturally. We decided to let these traces of doubleness subsist.

GOD

Paris, September 25
New York, October 14–20
Paris, October 29, 2002

Your first book (and hence your oeuvre as a whole) opens with God with a capital G and with the given name of the being whose "patronym" is to traverse your work. Moreover, twenty-six years after Le Prénom de Dieu *(1967)*, Beethoven à jamais *(1993) is subtitled "or the existence of God." With or without a capital G, he is by turns merciful, maleficent, benign or terrible, in the Rilkean sense: ". . . the howl of admiration of the stunted little human creature before God's enormous grandeur . . ." (p. 88);*[1]

---

[1] All page references correspond to the original, French editions of the works in question. A bibliography of Cixous's works in French, up to 2003, the year of the last interview in *Rencontre terrestre/Encounters*, and, where they exist, their English translations, is provided at the end of this translation. I am grateful to Marta Segarra, Eric Prenowitz, and Marguerite Sandré for their preparation of these bibliographies.

1

"Perhaps at that moment they saw this famous God, the one who almost doesn't exist, an unbearable, threatening vision . . ." (p. 52); "There was only God. God was necessary and He barely sufficed" (p. 120); "And God? As for the existence-of-God, that day they didn't manage to avoid it"; ". . . there was in the bedroom's entrails a need to run through God's possibilities . . .". These possibilities are then designated, detailed: "God was their moan of voluptuousness [. . .] a magic glove over the extravagance [. . .] the name of their astral offspring [. . .] the infrared eye" (pp. 91–2), etc. What do you see in this word set like the key signature – sol, ut, or fa – at the entry to all your books?

Only *you* could have seen what is plain as day, to the point where *It* is so present that It vanishes, like the light of day one doesn't see as Blanchot writes because one sees only day, in the day of the day; I want this pregnant, immersive presence of God, mine, not the God of Abraham nor of religions but somebody I call God to help me excuse and bear the miraculous and thus threatening side of life. God has been very "man" for me, since he was born to me, he's a god who was born to me [*qui m'est né*] (I hear *hyménée*) upon the death of my father. That day I said to God the Great: I deny you and take my father as God with whom to speak of god. I am never without (God) god, gods, one god, the god, mine, and I write with the help of god the mygod or the bi-god, but unconsciously. This god is the condition and the consent. You are quite right to see him as the key signature, of *sol* or of *fa* or of sky,[2] written at the entry to each of my texts. What is certain is that it's him, not me who sets the tone. The space of the secret within which I keep myself or am kept, and in which I

(Unless specified otherwise, all footnotes are the translator's additions. – BBB.)

  [2] *Sol* in French also means "ground," whence the play on *ciel*, or "sky."

am permitted, is constituted by this Being. It is something like the substance of my belief. If I fear a great deal, I doubt little.

Isn't it, in your eyes, particularly difficult to "speak" of your work? I use the verb in two ways:

(1) it is difficult "to speak about": that is, to produce a discourse-commentary on the blocks of discourse-fiction which are your books;

(2) isn't it also difficult to "speak," produce an oral discourse on a written discourse, because of everything that is found in the language and not found in the spoken word? So we first tried, as we shall see below, to "speak" this book, and the result was not very conclusive. When our interview took a turn toward the written, it worked better. In addition, your language is an idiom apart, and because of this it is spoken and written differently.

Back in Paris, October 29, 2002

Response "dreamt" – between New York–Newark–Chicago–Evanston–Paris – in the unfolding and refolding of secretly sacred places, as if a God or "the God" had "really and truly" walked in them in the present, elegant-hideous places lovely in their ugliness or lovely in their infinite purity, Cities, Cities, as Rimbaud would say, and for me Cities hence Temples, Ruins, books before the books – to the question "isn't it, in your/my eyes, difficult to 'speak'. . ." a question that I ask myself on my knees before these Cities that come from the most distant reaches of my memory, as if they wanted me to speak of them while daring me ever to have the necessary strength.

As for my work and taking into account the *terms* of your question:

"In your/my eyes," everything is difficult. Myopia, blurriness, diplopia, all the inexactitudes and insufficiencies that afflict my vision are, true, an insistent and constant factor in

3

the concrete and figurative, physical and philosophical difficulty of speaking as and in order to see, to say a seeing, to perceive [*percer-voir*], or *Persée-voir* [Per/see/us]. But what is "difficult" is reassuring and necessary, for it is what all literary works have in common: "difficult" to read [*difficilire*] in the first instance, always requiring the apprenticeship of a language (and of a way of thinking), of a language-thinking and providing food for thought. An apprenticeship that is in itself a state of reading. Di-fissile.

But you speak here of "*speaking*" as distinct from writing or reading, and I am with you, on several fronts. I myself "speak" my thoughts a great deal, in seminars: that is, I elaborate a kind of discourse intermediate between the spoken word, improvised, and a very particular kind of *oral writing*, engendered by the place and by my audience of researchers, already trained, adept, and practiced, as if for a form of music: consequently I take risks, I exercise the language, I play it more than anywhere else. Yet, were one able to compare and measure, the oral *fabric* is less dense and less tangled with depths than when I write. So I always feel that it's only in writing, on paper, with the pen, in that gesture and that temporality, that I succeed [*parviens*], that I *parleviens* [speak/succeed], that I reach the most unknown, the strangest, the most advanced part of me for me. I feel closer to my own mystery in the aura of writing it. When I speak (and I take pleasure in doing so) it's by force, hesitatingly, as if I were walking on air.

I can speak, or write, around my books, as if I skirted them, looked down on them, an approximation, I can – "translate" my own book into Oral form but it's just a translation in one or two voices: the book too is a translation, but more powerful, an orchestra. I add that I am not my own texts' best commentator. I am sometimes subjugated by the readings that are communicated to me. Yours has an absolute singularity, it is itself a work, and poetic. I recall I was all but overwhelmed

4

by the reading called *H.C. pour la vie*, when Jacques Derrida delivered it publicly at the 1988 Cerisy Conference: I felt myself "read [*lue*]", "seen [*vue*]," and "naked [*nue*]," taken by surprise, as if detected, as I'd never myself before seen myself, and I *recognized* myself with a kind of terrified admiration for the recognizer, literally: I didn't know *where* to hide, for my (unconscious) hiding places had been found, and I had no more *where*. In fact for myself I am hidden. Certain, very rare readings "dis/cover" me. Mireille Calle-Gruber's,[3] each time, is a shot of *over-excitement*, of childlike exaltation.

What to say about the alternation, the oscillation between "prose" and "poetry" throughout your books? Would you agree with the default generic definition that establishes difference and separation but also proximity, as between the two sides of a sheet of paper?

"The oscillation between prose and poetry" – I'm not sure I can make that work for me. What I agree with is oscillation, a word I like a great deal and which I feel. But prose-poetry, for me there's no difference. It seems to me that I write pro-etry or that in the text I play on all the registers and colors, deliberately. I don't think I've ever really "prosed."

*

Three years earlier we'd set off in a different direction because I wanted – the apparently linear route was an illusion but I didn't know this yet – to mark our path as best I could.

---

[3] Hélène Cixous and Mireille Calle-Gruber, *Rootprints: Memory and Life-Writing*, translated by Eric Prenowitz (London/New York: Routledge, 1997).

Paris, February 21–2, 2000

I thought that during the course of this interview we could simply follow the chronological order of your books' publication: that is, more or less the order in which I discovered them, from the 1970s onwards, as they were coming out. So here I opt for a chronological reading, aware nonetheless that we could easily envisage a different order, read the texts in reverse or independently of the chronology, beginning, for example, with the most recent ones, Or, Les lettres de mon père, Osnabrück, *and* Les Rêveries de la femme sauvage, *which bring together and refine most of the themes at work in the work overall.*

The reading disseminated in the "linear" and "chronological" reading (if it exists). Go-up-and-down, but like squirrels which make the top dance at the bottom. After all, this is what we do with all literary works. When I read Stendhal, I don't pay attention to the time, the dates . . . sometimes I might look at the "realistic" chain of events there, but it's rare. Thomas Bernhard, whom I will be visiting in my seminar, and to whom I often return, comes to mind as well: I believe he wrote his so-called autobiographical work rather late. Moreover the four admirable texts that describe the legend of the origins didn't obey strict chronological order but a necessity or an urgency from within the writing. "The order" of reading or writing is therefore a trompe-l'oeil, even if we discern in the depths broad generative movements, unplanned by the author, which forced themselves upon her so strongly that it is good for the passionate reader to track them.

(Let me add here – in a shameless afterthought, for this parenthesis is being inserted in 2002 – that a reading like yours is extremely rare: born at virtually the same time as the works, a sort of separate twin, unpredictable, and all the more extraordinary in that it has never lost heart, whereas one might have expected it to abandon its extraordinary accompaniment considering this peerless reader's age. I add to the

6

addendum that we have therefore gone our parallel ways without meeting up, you, me, in a space-time which was – is – the very substance of this world we call literature.

That a *meeting* should have occurred was the result of another series of serendipitous accidents. Let's say that we could have continued down our separate paths without this book having any reason to come into being. I have had some remarkable non-encounters: thus the non-encounter with Clarice Lispector, who was (still) living when I first read her and whom I never dreamt of meeting. There have been others. I have always considered the author to be someone dead with an apparent life.)

If one takes the field of literature in general, there are, however, works that develop along clearly marked lines, Joyce, for example. There, there is an order.

In the end the work will be a single letter with the date of one "long day" – century.

In the case of this interview, chronological order comes from the fact that I read your books, my contemporaries, as they appear, and so I perceive them not as an already constituted mass (which they are as well) but as a thread that lengthens, spins out, and also as a territory that enlarges itself via alluviation; therefore it seems to me difficult to cut a swathe through a work in the making, where each new link modifies, in effect, the organization of the whole.

*

Paris, February 21, 2000

For Joyce, it is indeed difficult to begin with Finnegans Wake.

One can, it's full of obstacles, but for a reader of texts, it's possible. On the other hand, in the development of Joyce's oeuvre, one sees clearly the passage from larva to butterfly, that is from the cumbersomeness of the classical form to the complete shattering of form in *Finnegans Wake*. But Joyce is a truly special case.

A more traditional reader may find it useful to begin with A Portrait of the Artist as a Young Man *or* Dubliners. *In order to learn Joycian . . .*

As a matter of fact, I don't know if one learns Joycian; in my opinion one picks up Dublinish, and the Joycian comes along later. Hence one learns the Dublin thematics or leitmotiv and afterwards one is prepared to enter Joycian. Before that, one is not in the Joycian, it's all very traditional. There's some work on the signifiers, all right, but it's hardly noticeable if one thinks, for example, that he's a contemporary of Proust. Joyce took great revolutionary leaps forward.

Did you begin your work on Joyce and your first book around the same time? Le Prénom de Dieu *appeared in 1967.* L'Exil de Joyce ou l'Art du remplacement *came out the following year.*

For me these two "books" were polar opposites. *L'Exil de Joyce* was a dissertation undertaken before I'd dared even dream about getting close to writing – I could find the date, in 1960–1, I believe – that seemed to me to be an enthusiastic critical reflection, disinterested or uninvolved with any subjective concerns of my own. I don't think I realized what intimate resonance the themes of *exile* or *replacement* had for me. My critic-eyes were trained on Joyce. Not without detachment.
I was making an effort.

What's striking is that one enters your language right away with Le Prénom de Dieu, *your first published book (become* Prénom de Dieu, *without an article, in the bibliographies). . .*

Ah! That's a mistake, a negligence on my part. I haven't reread those lists for ages. Thank you for telling me.

Right away, in this first book, you find your language, as if it had been there all along. Look at the first lines of the first sentence: "The flesh of my death is smooth and tender, nobody ever embraced me like you, it is all around me, a single enveloping, buoyant, imponderable caress, I am inside . . ." And the reader, too, is inside, a word which is to become the title of your next book[4] and first long text (so as not to say "novel," but we'll come back to this notion of genre). This first collection, Le Prénom de Dieu, *also contains texts whose syntax is more classical, somewhat in Kafka's line, and a male narrator. But this incipit of a first text brings the reader squarely into your language, the Cixaldian, if I may call it so.*

You notice how embarrassed I am, for it's a book I've never gone back to. In one of the manuscript volumes that are in the process of being classified before going off to the Bibliothèque nationale, I discovered a meditation on *Le Prénom de Dieu*, from a certain position of exteriority, which goes back a few years, seven or eight perhaps, I'm not sure. A friendly incident occurred, a remark Derrida made in passing, he was reading through certain of my texts, a reflection whose general idea was, I think, that everything was already present in *Le Prénom de Dieu*.

Yes, it's very striking, that's why I wanted to begin with it.

I no longer remember exactly how he put it, it was admiring, and because of it I wrote four or five pages, about my relation or non-relation with my texts, something which is

---

[4] Although *L'Exil de Joyce* (1968) was published next after *Le Prénom de Dieu*, *Dedans* (1969) was, in fact, the next book to be *written*.

9

over-determined, above all my non-relation, the distance I maintain from certain of my texts, especially the first ones: I recognize that I'm afraid of them. I'm afraid of them [*Ils me font peurs*], in the plural, they cause me several fears. One of these fears doesn't just apply to that book but to almost all my texts. I have a problem turning back, I don't read myself or only very rarely.

But one reads oneself all the time while one is writing . . .

Oh yes, of course! But as soon as a text is written and published, it goes off. It goes off, and I don't try to hang onto it. I hang onto it, or it stays with me for a few months, then it must go. Sometimes it tiptoes back, because it gets read by a researcher who asks me a few questions, but in general I keep my distance from it. So I'm reluctant to turn back, because in any case I need to move on, not read myself in the mirror: when one writes one doesn't read oneself as one looks at oneself in a mirror, it's not at all the same thing. Reading the book once it's weaned and published is like a mirror. If I read a book, I read it as a reader and to what was for me writing I apply reading, and this I don't like. So there's this resistance, but there's also that the first book I wrote got written in a sort of very *unheimlich*, strangely disquieting, mental atmosphere, in which the phenomenon of writing was for me monstrous, terrifying, vital but deadly, in which, basically, I couldn't and, moreover, didn't want to leave the grotto where all this was sublimating, where it was cooking its lava. So I had a feeling of being possessed, of being the object of a kind of possession, and of course it has always struck me that being possessed is also a form of dispossession: that is, that paradoxical situation where when one is possessed one is dispossessed and, at the same time, one is on the contrary dis-possessed of dispossession; truly nothing could be stranger. I've always had a sort of instinct of horrified repulsion with regard to those moments that totally escaped me, that happened within me, all the while escaping me.

You talk about it in the past. Are you saying things happen differently now?

I'm speaking here about those first texts that were demoniacal, that I had great trouble bringing myself to sign, of which I said that "It wasn't me who wrote them." Even this was a sentence I couldn't use because I couldn't say "me," it was much too complicated. They were texts written through me, unrecognizable to me, that were illegal, clandestine, not to say mad. And then that thing, that feeling of absolute non-legitimacy, got decanted. I no longer feel this almost shame at robbing myself in my absence – literally this was what I would think when I was writing my first texts: I'm robbing myself.

The writing itself allowed you to rid yourself of the "shame" connected with this dispossession?

I think it's simply the repetition of the act and the affirmation of the thing: I was so dispossessed by possession, possessed hence dispossessed, that I was clearly convinced that, just as writing appears, it could disappear, that I did not in the least have and could not say I had a writing-being. This not-having caused me terrible anguish, I told myself: *it* is going to go away, *it* happened, *it* came and *it*'s going to go away. I was much more tense, nervous, uncertain than now, when I tend to lean in the other direction: now I make the inverse projection: *it* won't go away, because *it* can only go away with my death. It is so linked to my life that, yes, it's going to go away after my death. But in the beginning my fear was that I would be abandoned. The "first" are therefore texts which were beyond me, in a way. The others too, but this feeling of fear of abandon and especially the conviction I had, that I still have, that it was stronger than me – I've always thought my texts were far stronger than I am – means I still have a holy terror of those texts and in a way they are off-limits to me. I have great admiration for those texts, it's kind of funny: I look at them as if from very far away and something of them stays with me: not at all what I wrote, but a state; a nocturnal state, a climate, some storms, heartache.

I was just about to ask whether you remembered the circumstances that impelled you write them.

Yes, that's what I remember rather than the book. Those nights full of dread are still with me. It was a nocturnal, insomniac, demoniac text. Fits. They subjugated me.

AND THE WHALE

Paris, February 22, 2000

Most of the themes are already present in that first book, Le Prénom de Dieu. *What sets it apart from the following books is the presence of a sometimes male or indeterminate narrator who later on gradually disappears, but your language is already there in all its strangeness, its singularity.*

That's what Derrida says, but also that it was pregnant with themes and motifs I had no memory of because, as I said, I hadn't reread it. The day he mentioned this, I shriveled inside. I didn't want to know. A holy terror. As well as a kind of dread at the idea that in those days I *knew* nothing, I didn't *know* how to write. It was like in that vision, which always appealed to me,

12

of the biblical prophet, the poor guy who suddenly hears the voice of God. I've always believed myself part of that scene. I've always had a spectacular and impressive vision of what happened for the prophets, Jonah above all. Probably because my German grandmother's family was called Jonas.[5] But I think that when I was little, I didn't make the connection. When I was ten I was absolutely fascinated by the Jonah story, but I was too young to realize that this was a clear case of over-determination. I mean, everyone was called Jonas: my father too was called Jonas, which I didn't pay attention to because no one ever called him Jonas, it was his Jewish name. My mother's family was called Jonas, that was the family name, but at the same time I didn't pick up on that, I left it far away, back there in Germany, and didn't realize its influence on me. But Jonah was a character I adored, in whom I saw myself completely. I told myself: "If I heard the voice of God, I'd jump straight into the whale!" That was my metaphor: I would wriggle like a worm, I'd get myself swallowed by a whale, rather than be the person who heard something so great big wet I had a vision of God, a vision that was auditory, it annihilated me, it transformed me into a speck of ear-dust. In fact, curiously, I believe I lived all the time as Jonah: when I hear the voice of the book, if I can say this, I have the feeling that I am an unworthy so-and-so who bolts into the whale's belly to flee the invisible Whale.

The whale is also the writing, Melville's white whale, the whale that gives rise to the writing, that whiteness that forces us, as Mallarmé implies, to blacken it?

I don't know why I've never adopted or integrated Melville's myth, perhaps precisely because I have my originary whale. And also because, in fact, the *Moby-Dick* story is a struggle

---

[5] "Jonas" is the French spelling of "Jonah."

between the man and the whale, and I don't like the assassination that goes on between old men and the sea. But it's an extraordinary fable, the whale which is itself a sea, the sea, the ocean within the ocean. So, all these first texts, I vividly recall the climate in which I wrote them, a climate of terror. That one, the most distant, I didn't write any more than *Dedans*. My first two books, I didn't write them.

You mean they came, they went through you . . . ?

Yes, they came and, what's more, in pieces. They're fragments, because I didn't think I was writing a book. I was writing things, what I was writing was in shreds, but shreds of my own flesh. There was no thought of putting them together or conserving them, it was really vomitings, confessions torn from me in spite of myself, I jotted down what happened, what turned up, humbly and without a project, without any project.

Already they were labeled as "novels," perhaps the publisher's idea?

False pretenses. They had no title. First because I've never "had" titles; these have always come along at the last minute, a long time after everything has been given to the publisher. When they are about to be published, since there's still no title, which is my problem right now, and each and every time, this for me is the hardest. I have no title. I await the help of the Great "Titrier," to gesture toward Jacques Derrida's mischievous text.[6] Therefore, what's on the cover is deceptive.

---

[6] "Titre à préciser" ("Title to be specified"), whose first section is entitled "Le titrier" ("The Titleer"), reprinted in *Parages*, edited by John P. Leavey, translated by Tom Conley, James Hulbert, John P. Leavey, and Avital Ronell (Stanford: Stanford University Press, 2010).

Whatever the publishers want to put, wanted to put, on the covers, in those days I let them do what they wanted, because I myself didn't know what I could have come up with instead. Those were still such traditional questions, I couldn't have cared less. "Novel" – this word is a fiction.

You use the term "fiction" to designate your most recent texts.

Yes, it's a simple, fairly vague indication because some people get confused if you don't set boundaries. I can see very well that certain readers would shelve my texts with "theory," as they say in the United States.

Because in addition you've published a considerable number of essays, which we won't even have space to touch upon here, nor on the theater either.

Because my fiction texts always have a philosophical "cast." Now I even see myself classified as a "philosopher" abroad. I resist that; it's not that I don't wish to be designated as such, or as an analyst or essayist or artist, these labels that come and go according to the circumstances amuse me. "Novel," on the contrary, doesn't fit any of the texts I've written, so that's fine, it's funny.

All the first books, Dedans, Neutre, Le Troisième Corps, Tombe, Portrait du soleil . . . *are nevertheless termed "novels" by their publishers, and have for a long time been perceived as such by critics, juries, etc.*

Or one could poke fun and say: Look what the novel was and what it's become, one could say that, in other words the complete opposite, why not? But I don't believe this makes much sense because the novel is, when it comes down to it, definable, so why not leave it its own territory and country? I like novels, even if I don't write them.

Do you share my feeling – quite widely felt, moreover – that we have entered the post-novel era, that the novel, at least in its canonical form, is no longer adapted to the lives we live? In demonstrating its obsolescence the Nouveau Roman was somehow the end of the novel, it rendered it impracticable . . .

It did in any case finish it off, if I may say so. But I think there are still two tendencies. Clearly today there are people who write "novels." And probably people will go on writing novels, probably because the uninformed and uncultivated public consumes novels. I think what we used to call "novels" will continue in a degenerated form, but also – this was already the case at the turn of the twentieth century – one can't write novels any more when one is in "writing' [*écriture*]. You can't say that *À la recherche du temps perdu* is a novel. Can't we say that in effect Proust and Joyce had already displaced tale[7] and narration, already disseminated, broken open, replaced subject and character? And proposed the Book in the role of main character?

Proust and Joyce shattered all that in their transgression of the boundaries of the novel, meanwhile taking it as frame of reference.

And it's been over and done with really for a century . . . or at least something else has sprung up to take its place, which

---

[7] In French, *récit*, a hard word to translate. It is strictly speaking an oral or written recounting of events, less formalized than a story, without the psychologically delineated characters one expects to find in a "short story," "novella" or "novel." "Story" and "tale, "the traditional translations for *récit*, can seem inadequate, because of evolving concepts of narratology and a less than perfect fit for literary terms and, indeed forms, between French and English.

can only be connected with the theme of writing [*écriture*] in the Derridean sense. The problem is one can't put "writing" on the cover of a book. The *thing* hasn't found its name and that's just fine.

The feminine pronoun appears in your second work of "fiction": Dedans.

I can't account in any simple way for this emergence. Let's say it's natural that what comes along as a pronoun be the feminine for me. I write with my whole body, so that it gets soaked up, inspired by breath and flesh in tune with the sex, more or less feminine, in tune with the experience of differences, affects, emotions, with an animal less male than female, so I can't cut myself off from the corresponding gender. It's *Le Prénom de Dieu* that is a hapax. I can't say why, and it had even slipped my mind that it was in the masculine. I don't know, and I can only hypothesize. Maybe I was this "it," a subject not masculine-virile, but pushed into the place of the son, it's a possibility. Or of the father? A young father? I don't know.

The father too is already very present. God is the name of the father . . .

Maybe I wasn't born yet, or maybe I was hiding something, or . . . no, I can't give any credible account of this, because I'm in the dark, furthermore, as I said, I didn't write those texts for publication, I wrote them because they were there. In the shadow of my father. The Shadow [*L'Ombre*]. The Nombrilic [*L'Ombrilic*]?

Were they there alongside, simultaneously with your research and the discoveries that you made in your dissertation, your work on

Joyce, or was it only once you had finished the dissertation that you "came to writing," to "fiction"?

The two countries were not connected. I had an outside world, social in a small way, I had the prowess to make my way around, but without believing in it at all. And I had my clandestine world, utterly shady, where my life in fact took place, or my death, I don't know which.

Your world sprang from the writing?

Not from the writing. The writing was the trace, the trail if you like, the tracks left by this dark life, which was an inner life, I wasn't trying to write. First of all I had no image of what would happen to me. The need to write and, rather than the need, the being condemned to write was there, *that*'s always been there. That's why I took a long time admitting it (as one admits a crime or a verdict). What survived, the flotsam, were these stories, but I'd been writing forever.

Since childhood?

My brother says yes, my loyal brother was telling me the other day that he'd kept my first novel, which I must have written at the age of ten. I haven't the slightest memory of this. He kept a notebook, which I've no desire to see, I'm sure it was devoid of interest, but he kept it, who knows what he was thinking. Me, I liked to scribble, but I idealized literature so – it seemed to me the divine world – that I couldn't imagine being part of it myself one day. I wanted to, but as a reader, so I never stopped reading. I wrote bits and pieces that all ended up in the trash, because, except for my brother, the people around me were more the throw-in-the-basket sort of people, everything I produced was instantly condemned. I myself

18

never stood up for what I was doing because I considered I was producing symptoms, I thought it was an illness, this itch.

Publishing and throwing away both allow one to clean the slate and move on. I've thrown out and burned lots of things and no longer have any regrets.

But I think that you were throwing away from *within* the work, because you were trying to write a book, with a book in mind, and me, no. That's why I haven't any trace of what I might have done, I didn't care, after all I wrote the way I ate, I was eating myself, secreting myself, excreting the waste, I had no thought of making a work of art, not at all, even if the thing inhabited me. In fact I'm almost diametrically the opposite from you, since I know that for you the time of living is a time of work: that is, even if you burn, destroy from within the work, it takes place inside and therefore it becomes part of the work, everything that gets destroyed still builds up the work. You are in pain like a woman in labor. Whereas I was not inside the work, and what's more I had no information and no intimations about my own destiny, so that I didn't even understand the signal that my thesis director gave me when I was twenty-three, twenty-four years old. My director, whom I loved unconditionally, was an old Sorbonne professor, enlightened, which is very rare, Jean-Jacques Mayoux, a man of tradition, a great man of letters, with a great sensibility and between us there was a very beautiful story, a kind of sublime love, I loved him not like a father, he wasn't paternal, well he was but intellectually, more like a tutelary divinity, a protector. *Dedans* is dedicated to him. In fact I wrote my dissertation in homage to Mayoux. I didn't want to do a dissertation. I started work on it, then right away I got a teaching position in a university, I was twenty-five, and when I saw what the university was like I said: "Oh this is hell, this will be the death of me, I've got to leave." I was innocent, and I feared for my soul, I said: "I'm going to lose my soul, this is the anti-soul, the a-culture, bourgeois society" and I left. I was an assistant professor at the University of Bordeaux and I resigned, in 1964 or 1965, for a year I had no position, no future, and I didn't really know what I was going to do, that's when I wrote *Le Prénom de Dieu*. And when I told Jean-Jacques Mayoux I had to resign, obviously this was blasphemous for the university, but he didn't reproach me, not at all. Very early on he'd already told me something, which I kept with me, which was a viaticum without my understanding it fully: "This dissertation, you have to get it done quickly, it's not important, what's important is that you write because you're made for writing." I was stunned.

ALREADY EVERYTHING WAS THERE

Still in Paris, February 22, 2000

This time you spent at university, your work on Joyce, have they helped you, in spite of everything, end up coming to writing?

If they helped me, it's paradoxical. The university having seemed to me like the Bastille of anti-writing. But I got along with Joyce also because he attacked all "universities," beginning with Ireland's reactionary Catholicism, one figure among many of the witch hunt against linguistic freedom. However, I believe everything comes from my father, from my experience with my father. The university appeared to me as occupied by frauds and hypocrites, right where I expected audacity and light and respect for difference. It was easy to pull the wool over my eyes when I was young, if I may say so,

20

precisely because I was the daughter of my parents, people whose sense of right and wrong was unaffected: that is, I didn't conceive people could build lives on lies, and I also believed in the word, I believed that what one said was a factor of truth.

Aren't such blows, lies, exile (Joyce's), etc., what make one come to writing – as a form of resistance?

I don't think I'm mistaken – I may, of course, be mistaken – but my version of my alliance for life for death with writing, as I've written in *Les Rêveries de la femme sauvage* and elsewhere, is that writing came into being for me in my earliest childhood. That is, in Algeria, in the tension between what was fine and noble, and which was based on the spirit of true integrity of my family – for my father, my mother, my grandmother Omi, my paternal grandmother too, were people who were utterly upright, and transparent, and the infamous things I saw the minute I crossed the threshold of our house, the social and moral baseness, the general practice of violence, contempt, trafficking, I could apply to Algerian society all the sins enumerated in the Circles of Hell (or in Joyce's Dublin), small, middling, big, sordid, the outside world was what it was, and I analyzed it implacably; I've never had blinkers in the City, never. I've always said, and on this point I get cross with everyone, that the blinkers – we put them on ourselves: when I was three years old I saw the world as it was, certainly by the age of four, I could read the signs, since my first brushes with history were in 1940–1. I understood everything, I saw everything, exactly what was at stake between humans, classes, races, religions, I saw it all. This made me revolt. I wasn't born a rebel, but by four I *was* outraged. They turned me into a rebel. It was an extremely virulent thing in me. The sudden onset of a storm.

Your parents didn't encourage this lucidity?

21

No, I think they were very innocent and they didn't see what I saw. I was myopic. My myopia gave me a strange clairvoyance. In fact I saw nothing, but I "saw" everything. I was in a state of unveiling.

That's one thread of your 1988 text with Jacques Derrida, Voiles, *that clairvoyant myopia. The most recent texts come back to the early ones. The* Comer *who appears in* Les Rêveries de la femme sauvage, *the writing that came and could go away again, and "the house ringed by, fenced with wire" turn up already in* Dedans, *everything that has been developed in these recent texts was there as if forever. It's striking to reread the early books today. Already everything was there.*

Yes. I've stopped worrying about this, and not only for myself, of course, but for any writer, I've told myself that in truth one only winds out and winds in, one has a sort of ball of magic silk thread, in the beginning one has all the threads and all one does is untangle them, wind them out and wind them back in; and not just that, for each of us has his or her own ball, but in fact we who write speak always of the same things, there's a big bouquet of the great human themes, which concern humanity in the broadest sense, the dead and animals included in general, through which all writers of all time have leafed, and the work is merely a variation on those themes. Perhaps it's strange to think that, but literature is the infinite of the finite. When I write I know ahead of time that all the roads I take, all the thought trails, Montaigne has been there already, for example, and I find that just fine, I rejoice in it, endlessly. I said Montaigne, but I could say others, we go over and over the same ground, this is a joy.

And are you conscious when you write today that you've already been over this ground yourself in another way, somewhere else?

22

Sometimes, yes . . .

That it was already in Le Prénom de Dieu, *in* Dedans?

I don't know what's in *Le Prénom de Dieu*. I haven't reread it and as I told you, the day Derrida brought it up, the ghost traumatized me and I told myself: I'd rather not know. Not turn back. I was afraid to remember myself. To gulp myself down whole!

In Portrait du soleil, *too.*

Definitely. Sometimes I have the feeling I'm writing something brand new, and then I realize I've already spoken about it, this happens to me. Obviously, in such cases I know the metamorphoses, new points of entry, point of view shifts, etc., can be the interesting part. So I don't worry, but I don't want to go back over what's done already. But as for *Le Prénom de Dieu*, which I've never reread, I also feel it's like the philosopher's stone, the magic scroll or the Torah, or some chest, something I had back then that I didn't know I had. What? A secret? A wound? A power? A panic? And this for me symbolically, in the imagination, has a force such that I must not touch it, it has to stay separate from me, buried, unknown. I realize that I have a sometimes very worrying feeling, which I admit to, a feeling of jealousy with regard to myself. I tell myself that once I was inspired, a little like in the myth of Samson. Look at Samson, blind. He'd been chosen by God – Samson Agonistes, Milton's (he only ever worked on this theme: on what was granted, and then lost, since he was blind, Milton, the greatest singer of sin; and I've always identified with this world of blindness, to which he was condemned, but which was also *granted* him) – it's the story of someone who had the light and lost it, since they

23

put out his eyes – in the Bible this isn't developed, it stays between the lines – and what is beautiful, profoundly moving, is to tell oneself that one can't lose the light unless one has already lost it. If Samson had his eyes put out, it's that he was already blind to what God had entrusted him with, his being chosen, he was already blind and he didn't see it. Blinded, at last "he sees." It's an utterly sublime story. As often in the Bible, the being wasted his inheritance, what was granted him. I recognize my destiny: I tell myself that when I was blind, I was chosen. When I didn't know, when I saw nothing, when I wrote without knowing I wrote, I was chosen, but now I "see": all that I can save of what I had and don't have any more is not to try to go and see what I didn't see and therefore saw without seeing.

Is it out of respect for the person one was that one doesn't turn back? For the person you were?

I am much harsher than that; I say it's out of jealousy. *Portrait du soleil* has come back into view for me because someone has written a thesis "on it." A very beautiful thesis. I said to myself: you *were* incredibly good. Or rather: "she" was good, the maker of this text, who is not me.

DWELLING

Still in Paris, February 22, 2000

You refer to Christa Stevens' thesis on Portrait du soleil; *in it she has unraveled all the threads and we see clearly that everything was already there.*

I tell myself: you'd better stay away from that.

24

It was while I was reading your latest books, from Or *on, that I recalled having read all that a long time ago, in another way, of course, because then it was much more deeply buried and hidden than today.* Ève, *the mother's first name, for example, back then seemed derived from myth. . . . Reading* Dedans *one didn't know that the encircled house was in Algeria, because this detail could pass for fictional.*

Yes, and it was fictional. That place, for example, was shelter to a large number of people. Each of them told his own tale, his own personal tale, thus fictional. To each her own fiction.

The house?

"The house" – there's more than one, there's "the house" or "the Clos" to which we return in our thoughts, we the family, each time we evoke it, immutable, eternal; there's also the house in metamorphosis, the house which comes back and becomes, in the texts, as subject to change as "the house" in my dreams.

Yes, for me it has become literature, but each of "us" has his or her own story, his or her version of this house, it's all a fiction, all a story, more or less elaborate. We are all stories. There's nothing but inventions. My mother, for example, gives me great pleasure (of which she's unaware because I'm unable to explain this to her) when, reading my latest books – that is when she forces herself to read them because she doesn't enjoy reading what I write, it doesn't much interest her – she tells me: "What an imagination you have! It's all made up, fantasies, stuff you've invented . . . ." She considers everything I write is made up. And I thank her. Because it's true. Of course, if you ask me, this fiction is as true as can be. But for her, it's mind-boggling. She says: "Truly, you've

25

always lived in another world." She thinks she has lived in the real world, and me in my imagination. Well that's fine. That's how it is.

Still, wouldn't you say that your writing is increasingly autobiographical, that you are closing in on real events? Put it like this: looking back one realizes the first texts, which appeared to spring entirely from the imagination, from a mythology (Ève, Georges, your father's name, Dioniris), were already autobiographical . . .

"Autobiographical" is a word I avoid. I've always been autobiographical, no more nor less than Montaigne or any other writer. "L'auto-" is always already other, translation has always already begun. That everything takes as its starting point the experience of the subject is something Montaigne boldly establishes in French literature. But so do Scève or Louise Labbé or François Villon or Viau or Proust or Stendhal. I don't see how one could write otherwise. Novels that don't spring from personal experience are shams. The distance between the source and the paper is more or less broad, and the period of writing, as of painting, changes, that's all. But I am always all three persons, first, second, third, the second is the first and the thirteenth returns and it is still the first.

You'll agree that people who go on inventing, fabricating novelesque characters out of nothing, even engaging in documentary research, if necessary, into other periods of history, are out of sync with writing's reality, its truth, its necessity for truth. Hence, no doubt, the surge in what has been called (clumsily, no doubt, but this isn't the place to forge new concepts in place of ones that are inadequate) "autofiction."

I've been really lucky – when I was little I had a tendency to think that I was unlucky, because I had a sense of the tragic,

I told myself: it's horrible the things that can happen. I saw the succession of exiles, deaths, massacres within the family, the brutally sudden death of my father; I would tell myself: how deep into despair can I plunge? It was endless. Now I tell myself that that was an extraordinary piece of luck: I was surrounded by human events; I experienced this very early on: that is, I could share the experience of humanity, crime, fiction, and punishment.

Would you have written otherwise?

I think at the outset one needs at least (1) the wound [*la plaie*] (2) the letters of the wound: *p, l, a, i, e* fading [*pâlie*], the call [*l'appelée*], the wound and the wheat of the wound [*la blessure et le blé de la blessure*]. Blood and tongue. One might say that writing begins embryonically. Writing is something one catches, like a disease, it catches us. Contaminates us. Counteracts us. It's so over-determined. There aren't a lot of people who write-live, even if there are lots who want to write. This is a choice, but a choice imposed on you. The only way to write is by doing nothing else: your whole life gets sucked in. I think that most people must dimly feel this and say . . .

That it's dangerous?

That it's dangerous, and at the same time people who believe they choose writing don't choose it, they are chosen. But certainly when one is not designated, called, one is not going to volunteer for an undertaking that costs you your life.
As you yourself know-live.

*

Le Prénom de Dieu, *as we've seen, was a book whose secret, whose trouble, it is better not to unveil. Following it, you published*

27

books that could be read at that time in all directions, like poems. Do you accept that one can read them like that?

Absolutely. I do this myself with the works I love. Of course there are hundreds of possible readings, I may read the pages in numerical order, but very often when I'm following the thread of the book, even while I'm reading, I add to it, I make forays, breaches, I backtrack. I think I have a good memory for literature, the texts are so alive for me that they are as present in my mind as the people I love, always. I spend a large part of my life with books as people, as companions, friends, and each time that I withdraw into myself, that I am alone with myself, I live by having all around me these people-books I know by heart. When I read, I do the sort of reading you refer to: I pick up this or that work I know well, and I go straight, right away I head for the place that resonates at that moment with my subject, and the conversation starts up again.

You know how to find this place, from living with the book?

Yes. And besides for me that's what a work is, it's a country and one stays in this or that part of it, in this or that garden, or park, one goes up this street, down that one, one has already lived in that hotel.

And the regions correspond to one another . . .

A book is just a vast depth, and what the book wants is for the reader to spend as much time with three pages as with a whole book. Every page is a book. My books are written like forests and mines. Proust would say: hotels, cities, cathedrals, one can read them the way I like to, all the time, read again-read forgetread [*oublire*] abolishread [*abolire*] read once more for the first time.

Of course there's a "narrative" or a "guiding" thread in any volume, which is simply the order of the pages, even when these have not at all been written in the order in which they find themselves assembled. And your books, especially those from the 1970s, can be entered in many places, their structure permits this. One can read them linearly, but they also allow an exploded reading, as one reads poems in a collection. And in the first of these texts, it seems to me that these disjunctions are very clear. Furthermore, when one writes, one reads the texts that help one write, and one must go and look for this or that page which will help us, that we need in order to write.

Yes, I think so too. One reads the texts that interpret our moods, the books that correspond, that write us, friendly *or* adversarial companions. To read, and feel oneself read is a pleasure. Readers are not necessarily specialists, or practicians of literature. But they're happy to see their feelings depicted, as I am when I read, and a voice speaks up within me, saying: that's me there, you who know me even if I don't yet know you.

Any reader can get into the act and becomes a writer, at this or that moment, by reading the appropriate text, the one that will make him or her write. One might also say that any reading is a form of writing, since one rewrites the text according to one's own experience, what our mind pictures as we read.

WITH

Paris, February 21–2, 2000

You've had a fairly strange passage from publisher to publisher?

Yes, that can be explained very easily. My first book was my thesis, which Grasset published, and at the time I was already writing, I'd written some small things, *Le Prénom de Dieu*, *Dedans*. The publishing world was wide open for me at the time.

Your work was an immediate critical success, on the part of some particularly influential critics.

True. But I didn't pay attention to those sorts of things. So I had given my thesis to Grasset, and on the other hand I was going to create the collection "Poétique" at Le Seuil with Gérard Genette and Tzvetan Todorov, in 1968. I had something with Grasset, something else with Le Seuil. With Grasset everything went smoothly right from the start. Even if they were irritated when I left. Their welcome was very warm, Yves Berger, Bernard Fasquelle took the book (*Le Prénom de Dieu*), a "crazy" book, and *Dedans*. I published those books "looking the other way" because I didn't think they were books. At the time, I moved ahead backwards, like Perseus, the books were the Medusa for the Perseus who was me. Plus for a while I was a kind of androgyne, or at least so I seemed in the view of certain people who were close to me. Thus Jean-Jacques Mayoux, my dear thesis advisor, used to call me "Theseus [*Thésée*]" Since this name had a feminine ending, I got used to it. That's when Derrida entered the picture. In those days I had friends in the world of Paris think-ers, among whom – this was really a totally amazing series of coincidences – were Jacques Lacan and Jacques Derrida. I met them the same year, I think it was in 1963, maybe even before, in any case 1963 at the latest, in completely different ways.

Through writing too?

It was because of Joyce. Maria Jolas introduced me to Lacan. In the 1930s Eugène Jolas created the journal *Transition*, in which he published Ezra Pound, Joyce, etc. The Jolases were philanthropists and genial amateurs (like the bookstore Shakespeare & Company). With great respect and generosity the Jolases had helped Joyce and his family. Maria kept track of the sad fate of Lucia, who ended her days in an English psychiatric establishment. They were somehow the "guardians" of their "brother," in the best sense. Jean-Jacques Mayoux had already written about Joyce and knew Maria Jolas very well; she was a close friend; he introduced us, she liked me a lot. One day someone asked her to recommend a scholar to initiate him into Joyce's work. This "someone" was Lacan, of whom I'd never heard. I meet him. And there, with Joyce, you have the beginning of a stormy simple and complicated friendship, which continued to Lacan's death. So there was Lacan, through this extraordinary Joycean connection, and a totally unpredictable series of events. Also, at my ex-husband's instigation, I'd met Derrida: they were candidates together for the philosophy Agrégation.[8] My ex-husband, in the course of one of our innumerable theoretical quarrels, had exhorted me in more or less these terms: "Go and see my classmate Derrida then; tell him I sent you, he's going to tell you what you're up to is mad." I wrote a letter from my Arcachon hole-in-the-wall, to Derrida, whom I "knew" from his texts, the very first ones he wrote. But the primitive scene of what was to become the most powerful intellectual and most inseparable tie and friendship of my life-as-writing had occurred several years earlier, in 1955. Arriving in Paris from Algiers, I was eighteen, and in my wanderings at the Sorbonne, I'd "seen" Derrida take his Agrégation oral exam. Without knowing either Derrida or the Agrégation. I listened to him, from the back

---

[8] The "Agrégation" is a highly selective French university examination.

31

row of a lecture hall, without seeing his face. However, what I heard struck me as the real thing [*cela même*]. From then on, I read him in journals as soon as he appeared. He spoke my language.

Even before the publication of his Grammatologies *then?*

I'd read his first texts in the journal *Critique*. I wrote him a very formal letter and he responded equally formally, giving me a rendez-vous in a Paris café, saying he'd hear me out but that he didn't know Joyce, etc. Jacques Derrida has himself told the story of this meeting, and the ones after it, in his text *H.C. pour la vie*. In 1963 we met up again. I was raving [*délirais*] my life then. I came to Paris to see Jean-Jacques, my advisor, I had friends in very different groups, foreigners dreamers exiles. Cortázar, Vassilikos, Fuentes. . . And in the darkest and most modest corner of all, someone to whom I owe far more than I will ever be able to acknowledge, who was for me the figure of the poet-survivor, the survivor despite himself, Piotr Rawicz, a saint without insignia, a bit of refuse from Auschwitz. Then there was the other world, the University, starting from the time when Jean-Jacques took me on at the Sorbonne, I had several worlds that didn't communicate, sporadic so to speak. I was there ecliptically. When I began to write, I suspected myself of alienation, in fact I was convinced of this. In a moment of anxiety, I showed Lacan a few traces: "Does this mean I'm mad?" Lacan said yes. "Of course, it's clear, who else writes such stuff?" Derrida, to whom I "submitted" what became *Le Prénom de Dieu*, which I unveiled like a plague or a leprosy, thought I was in perilous straits. He was brave enough to encourage me in the danger. Both thought, each in his way, that I had a future in madness.

Writing is sublimated madness . . .

But neither of them knew very well where I was headed. Derrida spoke about this at Cerisy. He had the comic kindness to say how he'd told himself: "But who on earth is she, what's she up to? She's crazy, she's going to get herself killed . . . it's demented, etc." He was at once both appreciative and anxious, telling himself that he wasn't sure that I'd end up . . . where? that I'd come to a good end?

In those days I had my look of normality, which was my "brilliant" university persona, where I demonstrated that I was a being capable of socialization. I mean, I was already a professor. So I entrusted *Le Prénom de Dieu* to Derrida. As he tells it – I didn't think he'd ever tell it – he paints himself as he was, Rousseau-Montaigne, more or less concerned about the situation. "What on earth's this torrent sweeping over me, here?" He told me: "But it's Artaud." A sort of "Alas!" I'd never read Artaud. I went off to read Artaud. When he said "Artaud," it was ambivalent, it was: "I don't know if it's brilliant, but I know it's delirious . . . ." But he urged me to publish: I gave it to Grasset, to Yves Berger, and in five minutes Yves Berger agreed. Same thing for *Dedans*, which I was a little embarrassed by, aware that I hadn't written a book but a mangled "thing." It's a little the same state of mind as that in which I took to theater: a "this isn't me." Someone wrote me things, I had visions, there were scenes that I scribbled down during the year, on scraps of paper, the year made a packet. Suddenly this was called *Dedans*. Through Yves Berger, Grasset published me without the least hesitation and without delay.

All the same these weren't easy books . . .

That's what I tell myself. It was very honorable on their part. Into the bargain I won the Médicis Prize whereas I was in my own inner world, and I didn't have the least idea of Paris or of prizes. I was a Papua, I didn't know where I was, what I was doing. I had been "taken into the fold." Gala Barbizan, who took the part of Mme de Warens[9] in my story, liked me. But that's as far as it went.

In those days, the Médicis Prize was still prestigious.

The jury was indeed textually very engaged. But I was so much elsewhere that I would have been capable of committing a kind of suicide. I was absolutely not part of that world. There were parties and I wasn't there, I was in the hospital, out of it; I didn't see where I was headed, I saw a pit in place of my life. And then I saw "Paris" for six months, Proust's Paris, the Paris open to its initiates, the universe of publishers, and so on, and I realized that there'd been a strange moment when Papua and Paris had met. "I can't 'be' in this world I told myself, I don't belong to the world of Parisian cocktails, I belong to the world of bestial angels and demons," I knew it. In this world-Paris, there were certainly some extreme sensibilities, some beasts holed up in their lairs like Piotr Rawicz, but rare. I left that world and in no time I wrote *Le Troisième Corps* and *Les Commencements*, which I gave together to Grasset. Graciously they published them, but I was told: "What you write is not quite our sort of thing, do you know what you are up to? You aren't going to win the Médicis Prize every time and we can't do too many bizarre books." Nicely, this wasn't a criticism, it was objective. I am told: "We'd like you to share, all by ourselves we can't support work like yours." They suggested a division, half Le Seuil half Grasset, since I'd had propositions from Le Seuil from the start. I'd published *Prénoms de personne* with Le Seuil in their "Poétique" collection, but someone

---

[9] Gala Barbizan was one of the founders of the Médicis Prize. Madame de Warens was a benefactress of Jean-Jacques Rousseau.

had the bad idea of asking me to change something, and I'd answered, "If that's how it is, I'm leaving." This is past history. Whereupon my publisher Grasset suggests that part of the time I go to Le Seuil. And I answer: "If that's how it is, I'm going to Le Seuil full time." In retrospect this all makes me laugh, I understand the reasons of each person in this comedy, my pig-headed self among them.

SPEW INTO THE SEA

New York–Paris, March 29, 2001

Aside from the fact that they appeared the same year (1970), what do these two extraordinary books, Les Commencements *and* Le Troisième Corps, *have in common for you, first of all in their circumstances? Did you write them together, or one after the other?*

Le Troisième Corps and then *Les Commencements* was the order in which they threw themselves at me at the time, in the same Season, really and truly thus: like Paradise and the Inferno, as Paradise is the Inferno, as the Inferno is the lost Paradise; but not together, thrown, one after the other. Very fast, very violently, and I was helpless to stop them.

Their "circumstances," you say: as if you sensed they were caused, surrounded, by circumstances, circaused, provoked. So they were, provoked first one and then the other, and rose up like provocations; provoked by raw, brutal perturbations around she-who-was-me. I've reread *Le Troisième Corps*, I skimmed through it again not long ago because it was about to be translated. *Les Commencements* never. I'd be scared to lift the lid of it. It's a seething cauldron, writhing with little dragons.

What they have in common: the spurt. Their being spewed

out, as when one sobs or, the contrary, as when one hemor-
rhages. The raw wounds caused by the people around us,
which is-was only the archetypal human constellation. In
those days I was living through primitive experiences, I was
finding out about assassinations among people who are close,
the prodigies of egoism the blindness the appetites I was like
a child at the breast the saint the signing [*au sein au saint au
seing*], I was finding out about weaning and separations, a uni-
versal experience. Struck I struck back.

Some years earlier I'd already lost everything and especially for a time my mind and that seemed like a preparation
for other beginnings. So: I entered, I was entered, I had taken
my first steps in the passion that awaited me, and I've never
left, I am there, and I was at the beginnings of the forest,
ablaze, those beginnings which as you know catch fire right
in the middle, or, as Kafka would say, in the holy of holies.

In *Le Troisième Corps* I explored with jubilation all the
trances, transpositions, transgressions, transfigurations which
are generally veiled and pushed into the thought-cupboards,
I opened up and I saw again how my father was a stork for
instance and how my mother has always swarmed, I went
through the cracks, the in-between-zones, where species
go to ground, enter, and make copies of themselves, and of
course all these realizations of our metamorphoses can only
take place in the first instance bodily.

Yet between these two books there was, not to beat around
the bush, a fracture, a time of "death," not many weeks but
profound like a voyage during which memory stops, the self
is engulfed, a hospital coma. I'm writing this because I know
that you yourself have experienced some of that. Never mind.
The upshot was a disaster but also a completely unexpected
melting away of inhibition, doors and eyelids stripped away
for a few weeks, and hence great surges of visions, sentences,
illuminations that made me die with laughter and anger and

36

which I noted without pity either for me or anyone else. A clairvoyant, hence cruel period. What came out of it was *Les Commencements.*

As for their content, their themes, might one say that they have in common or sparked the invention – alongside Blanchot's – of the neuter, this third person of the body which you come back to in 1972 with Neutre, *precisely?*

In the "content" – which therefore it was not – was the discountenancing, I don't know about this, I didn't think that "the invention of the neuter" had already taken place (this happened in 1969), but rather the inscription of the third person, the chance comer, the other, the haunter, the uncontrollable, the overflowing [*débordant*] (I should write this more precisely: the *débordans*[10]). But this apocalypse of our beyond, the beyond that goes along beside me and into which I pour and supplant myself, urged by Thou, saint, him, body of my body, certainly made a place for this neither-this-nor-that which haunted me and has haunted me my whole life in order to have it at last be narrated by a trickle of voices forty years later *the day I wasn't there.* This neuter, this knot in my memory, is in no way affectively neutral, it is my failing, my third body known as dead, but dead ahead, my fault.

Paris, February 22, 2000

Before publishing Tombe, *with Le Seuil, you gave* Portrait du soleil *to Maurice Nadeau's collection, "Les Lettres nouvelles."*

Yes, here's what happened: I gave the two books, *Les Commencements* and *Le Troisième Corps,* which admittedly

---

[10] *Débordans* combines *déborder,* "overflow," and *dans,* "in" or "into."

weren't in the least Grasset's cup of tea (tea = *thé*, *t'es* [you are], *tais* [be quiet], *taie* [pillowcase + veil or leucoma on the eye], etc.).

And with regard to the previous work, these constituted a new threshold, a new stage.

Yes, I was really entering my own territory, if I may say so. So at Grasset, they say: "This is too much for us. What's more you are publishing two books"; and I grant you, they'd published two books at the same time, which was a lot. And, as I said, I turned to Le Seuil. And I gave *Tombe* to Le Seuil, but in the meantime there was this absolutely crazy story, about *Portrait du soleil.*

Portrait du soleil is an extravagant text, an eruption. I offered it to Gilles Deleuze, my friend and often fellow pro-testor (we were part of Michel Foucault's GIP, the Groupe d'informations sur les Prisons [Prison Information Group]), to read, it was the day of a protest, a mob, violent, clubbed, the police charged, we were separated, I lost Deleuze, I am without news of him until the next day, he'd done time in the police station, he comes out, unharmed luckily, and tells me on the phone that my text has hightailed it, he has no idea where. I didn't have a problem with that. In those days the appearances and disappearances of my texts were frequent and uncontrollable, I considered that the loss was a fate like any other. I didn't have a copy (this was in that adventurous period before photocopies, when manuscripts were forever in danger of shipwreck). End of story. Two months later, a phone call from Gallimard. Roger Grenier thanks me for having sent a manuscript, which he has read and recognized, for even without a title and author's name, it's easy to see that I'm the sender. I am terrified and vexed: what! already I am imitable and imitated. I tell him I didn't send anything.

Furthermore this business of anonymity – what nonsense. Sorry, it's not mine. My interlocutor reads me a few lines and it is mine! It's *Portrait*. It seems the police station forwarded this protest march detritus to the most publisher of publishers. All beat up. What a great story. Whereupon, despite the warm "acceptance" of the manuscript found in a police envelope, I'm unable to accept this acceptance: I am with Le Seuil. Enough challenges. Upon which they suggest skirting the rivalry scene by publishing the thing in an allied but modest but noble publishing house, Nadeau's "Lettres nouvelles," and thus *Portrait* gets off the streets and out of the paddy wagon and finds itself welcomed with open arms by a fine place.

OFF AGE'S SHORE

New York, May 2–Paris, May 9, 2001

Following the astounding editorial meanders of the manuscript, there's the story of Portrait du soleil*'s reception; what do you think of Christa Stevens' thesis, I mean this critical reception at such a remove (thirty years later) from the text's publication?*

When Christa reads *Portrait du soleil* she becomes reading incarnated, she makes *Portrait* return toward me, makes it a revenant. But I don't feel a sense of distance, or being far from it, at all. Simply a kind of transfer: she sends me the Portrait of Christa. She offers me its today.

What your question brings to mind: a reflection on the "time-figure" of the work as a whole, as oeuvre. I seems to me that I live/see my work from two points of view (for this, invent the verbs livesee, seelive [*vivoyer, vivoir, voirvivre*], etc.).

39

First of all, I think on the one hand of "book" – as a singularity; on the other hand I think of "work." A "book" has a date, an inscription in a linear timeline; in these terms *Portrait du soleil* (1974) is very distant indeed.

But I have a tendency now to consider my texts as gravitating toward a "work," in the vague circle of a whole otherwise-distant from me: the books are all letters mailed to the future, and read in my absence, after me (me alive or me dead). In this future which is that of reading, time is annulled and *Portrait du soleil* is no further away in perspective than *Déluge* (1992).

One comes across this idea again in Portrait de Jacques Derrida en jeune saint juif (p. 57): *"The writing surarrives and puts time out of joint, derails it, it makes its entry as the past-already while holding out the promise of the already-future that it is, that it will be. It makes your head spin, this whirligig of dates, pursued by anticipatory memory: . . . ."*

What age is a book? What is an age? What is age? What age am I? I no longer know. Books happen off age's shore. Besides writing for a long time about a disturbing experience is a disturbing experience for the person one is in "real life," for each book, past-present, can be lived in the present the ephemeral present, as time-stopped, or as a "death sentence [*arrêt de mort*]."

But everything that I'm saying here quickly and badly demands a complex analysis of my relationship to memory-and-forgetting, and to "coming back" (in which I am presently involved for my text *in progress*).

(*N.B.* added on November 13, 2002: the text in question was *Manhattan: Lettres de la préhistoire*, which was to be nameless until the last moment, existing as *Le Récit.)*

Very quickly books distance themselves from me, to find

40

that time-without-date in which they remain, utterly eluding period. Hence I read Stendhal or Dostoevsky as contemporaries, with one another, with me, with you. This is all an optical effect.

Everywhere one finds this notion, this sensation of speed, of rushing; for example, in Déluge *(1992), which you've just mentioned: "Fast, faster, for I have to go faster than myself in speed and light . . . History, already, which was taking place a little ahead of me, thinking in advance of my thinking, hand in advance of my hand, illumination before light" (pp. 208–9). An instant ago you were comparing* Déluge's *distance from you to that of* Portrait du soleil, *written twenty years earlier. If I do have a good sense of your work as a whole, I also follow it from book to book like a chain in which I seek to find in each link an inkling of what is to come, if I can put it this way. Which doesn't, of course, prevent the interpolations and projections. We are at work here in a perspective both chronological and retrospective.*

Books, most of them, are enveloped in a kind of immemorial-ness, even if they refer to dated historical events. *Portrait du soleil* I could (have) write (written) tomorrow. And who knows whether I'm not going to be inspired to do so. . .

N.B. I wouldn't say this in the same way of all my texts. Some of them, I would no longer write, they were moments. Others are time's roots, they will send up shoots.

In this Portrait *we find two characteristics of the books of this period: first the absence of chapters in the usual sense, replaced by white space between the blocks of text.*

I like this remark, because it makes me aware of something I've overlooked, this organic fashioning whose necessity is fashioned behind my back. In a certain way the volumes, the shaping of them, is what I think least about. What I do know that I do deliberately is at times a fragmentation, a chopping up, but most of the time the text's breathing pattern imposes itself on me, while I dream-write. Now if instead of chapters there's a flow this is the reflection of a state (of which I have no organized, lucid memory but I've a state-of-memory) – this would be like a passion, a gust, with my senses I "remember" a swelling of angers or of a sort of black enthusiasm, in the etymological sense of this word, the sorts of heavy seas one can't interrupt, and which make themselves felt with very violent affects. One cannot cut the speech of the storm.

This confirms what we felt: the books from this period are storms, the most recent, including Déluge, *despite its title, are chopped up into precise chapters into which the flood is canalized. Probably – this is a working hypothesis – something of the violence of the initial upswell has decanted itself.*

Second characteristic of Portrait du soleil, *already the case, as we saw, in your first book, the unexpected presence of a masculine narrator: "If there was a hole in memory I would fall [je tomberais] into the infernal nest that the bi-God fashioned: I would be crushed bones, and I would be like a man broken and dying, crushed by the infernal times, seeing before his eyes at the moment of death the life he might have had . . ." (p. 70).*

The presence of the masculine narrator, who is more precisely a "like," is a trance, a state of possession. Let me add, with neither doubt, nor certainty, that the intensity of this presence says something about my porosity, in those days, as regards the archetypical masculine structure to which I would compare myself, use myself, amuse myself. (N.B. I'm not generalizing: I was knocking as at a door against the typically masculine part of a man, which, as far as that goes, is in no way typical, repetitive, or reproductive.) So it was also an entangling, a determination, and a working out of my own masculine part on the scene of fleeting or insistent confusions, embraces, transmutations – I also feel in that sentence an identification-compassion for the dying man, as if the character dying was a man full of regrets.

The extract I quoted above has a verb that's very present in your writing in those days, so much so that it even becomes the title of a book, a least in one of its accepted meanings: the verb tomber *[to fall], as in* Tombe *[fall, tomb] published by Le Seuil that same year, 1973. In light of what you have said about* Commencements, *should one read into this recurrence the metaphor for a state of imbalance?*

I wasn't thinking about it at all any more, this "*tomber*" – although God knows I "tombe /fall" these days, in spite of myself and understanding as I do so that I am "miming" a state of reversal. You are right, this vocable was the clue to a proximity with the abyss – and thus with the edge, vertiginousness, falling. And then the sound of this terrible word falls too, *tombe, bombe, sourd, lourd* [tomb, bomb, deaf, heavy], and then I go about carrying a tomb on my back, my father's, like my snail shell, and then I found strange that in the cemetery nothing falls less than a tomb, and in action one falls in love, but upwards. *Tombe* weighs and fascinates. *Tombe* is very violent, when it comes out of your mouth, and at the same time it begins with *ton* and then falls in tone. Yes, I had a psychic *tombe* which drew me. A fear of the attraction. Imagine a siren. The silent siren one fears (not) to respond to.

PERUVIA[11]

Paris, May 2–9, 2001

Another thing is that Tombe *has a new setting: Peru, Mexico even, the voyage-clairvoyance. Is this a wish for the "novel"?*

(Response following the invisible Paris–New York–Roosevelt Island line – a lightning-fast connection, I savor the transcontinental conversation that knows neither time nor distance, but if such a conversation can exist, surely it is only between you and me, it has been going on already forever, going on between us, at a time when, before our first meeting, Avenue René Coty (what was the date?), the encounter had already happened, and this thanks to literature.)

So: *Tombe*, I'll speak of it from a distance, for it's one of the books that was for me "venomous," vein, venereal, *Weh* (pain). You are probably right to imagine a desire for the "novel." In any case there was a wish or rather an apotropaic necessity: the seething, the purulent, what was incandescent to say, I could only approach veiled in linen – the shroud[12] of letters – that safeguarded the skin of the heart. As in the case of *Neutre*, *Tombe* circled around the inavowable, the unmournable. I must have carried the facts right to the decor (you mention a "new setting") which transfigures, and invents a ceremonial as if to invoke a kind of red magic. Peruvia (I'd totally forgotten), I'm delighted that it seems like Mexico to you.

There's a mask. I'll tell you later, next year, where Peruvia

---

[11] *Peruvia*: the French title of this section is *La Péruvie*, a coinage that combines the words Peru and *vie* (life), and whose first syllable also echoes the French word for father, *père*.

[12] *Shroud*: in French *linceul*, whose root is *lin*, linen.

is. In the meantime it is of course in the play of signifiers: *Pérou, Père, perdu, vie* [Peru, father, lost, life], etc.

Some of the referents or ceremonial accessories come also from the Greek archives, of the Adonis cult, from antiquity's thematic of death and resurrection, from the mythic associations with a certain kind of vegetation, from a world where celebrations exist from the entrails of the earth right to the harvest. In which one finds again – just travel along the subterranean rivers – Mexican myths and rituals.

New York—Roosevelt Island–Paris thread, March 10, 2001

I'm searching for my 1997 agenda to find the exact date of our earthly meeting – our terrestrial encounter – at Françoise's; in any case it was some time in September 1997 – as for my first encounter with your books, that takes me back to 1973! (As a matter of fact, it was with Portrait du soleil *and* Tombe, *which I have in their original editions, now unfindable.)*

I'm the one who is delighted by this close conversation at a distance & by being with you in Peruvia (I've taken some wonderful trips in my life but never all the way to where the father lives, in Peru[13] – I've never discovered where).

*After asking my last question I came across [*tomber sur*]this sentence again in your "Vues sur ma terre": "I say the word 'tombe' somewhat cautiously but nonetheless without falling [*tomber*]" (in* Hélène Cixous, Croisées d'une oeuvre, p. 237).

Let me continue and restate, still somewhat confusedly: in Tombe *one finds Dioniris Adonis Peruvia Pergamon Persephone once again, hence a wish for the novel and the circulation of myths (on the subject of an allusion you write ". . . he compares her to a serpent with several jaws to his own heart turned against him to*

---

[13] Peru: a play on the sounds of the French, *Pérou* (*père* [father] + *où* [where]).

45

a Mexican sacrifice at which he seems to be the priest, the heart the heart torn out . . .," p. 95). This personal mythology has an Egyptian side of course if we follow the links: death of Dioniris – arrival in Peruvia – destiny and the pen – and what is veiled . . . the torn-out paper, the pen and our sheets (p. 101), the embalming of the mummy, the unwinding of the bands, themes that reappear in La, *and we also find:* "Tombe *is only a weak emanation of the book of books*" *(p. 101),* "We will write the book that's beyond the book" *(p. 104), etc. It is also a first great travel book, before the* "Book of the Dead," *which* La *also is.*

Reacted to the lovely expression "terrestrial encounter" by the following daydreamt-thought: that an encounter can only be called "terrestrial" by making the transparent wings of the Encounter, the Previous – and promising – one, tremble. And, as a result, "terrestrial" (I always love this word, it contains everything) is borne aloft, to the plane of air where its *t, t,* drops, and all that remains is requiem splendor.

There's only an encounter, a meeting, if this meeting took place before the meeting, which may be not be followed by any terrestrial meeting (so Akhmatova used to sigh for all the friends whom she had (n)ever-met).

"Answers": Dioniris: Oniria, god of Umbria – the country of dreams. Adonis, Adonaï, all we know of him *Venus and Adonis* (Shakespeare), the myths and rites of Adonis, Peruvia Pergamon = parchment (lambskin from Pergamon) + Troy; Persephonia from Oniria, land of dreams. And Persephone in Greek mythology is a sort of female Adonis. Adonis, Adonia, land of Adonis, Agony, etc., whose name *in French* relaunches the hypermasculine. Père, Perseus. Phone, Faun.

Egypt: has always haunted me. As if I were of it. As if I came from it. As if I believed in Osiris (I do, I am Isis picking up the pieces of my father). Funnily enough, I'm thinking that if the mother "in" you seems incompatible, unlike my mother-daughter, the father within you on the other hand sleeps and wakes, just like mine in me. Your father gave you the shibboleth toward me, did he not? He spurs you on and causes you anxiety, like mine, only different. The young-dead-father, youth eternal, the eternal *je-naisse*.[14] The mummy: you make me notice that it has been present, always from the beginning. Its bands bind it to my soul. This violent method of conservation that transforms the body into a dry book waiting to be read so as to come back to life.

The book of books, the book toward which I look, even in the book I'm writing now, flits off ahead of me, like the sacred animal that makes all the impure knights gallop toward mortal purity (see the Grail or Saint Julian the Hospitaller). The most astonishing is that en route, during the pursuit, stumbling along, I write this or that book that I couldn't write (this is the case for *Le Jour où je n'étais pas là*) but the Ultimate one – I know it and I'll die before it, in front of it, but without having renounced. Moreover, sometimes this pursuit, already begun, already *Dedans*, already *Tombe*, so tires me that I want to die = sleep. Perchance to dream that I write it at last? My fear: my eyes, which at the moment seem to preach a sort of abandon. I don't want to give up.

OF MAPS & OF PRINTS

To what extent is this extraordinary travel book, Tombe, *linked to your own geographic voyages? One feels the erudition being, shall we say, tested by geographic reality . . .*

---

[14] In French *je-naisse* sounds like *jeunesse*, "youth," as well as *je naisse*, "to be born," in the first person of the subjunctive.

Voyages: what a fascination I have for this word (*Voy* = see!) (and there's *age*!) which I love (it comes up thematically in *Benjamin à Montaigne*, whose proofs I have just corrected) and which is not my word. Not my word not my voyage. I love voyagers. But the voyage is my mother, my love, it is part of me (my daughter) but not me: my numerous voyages pursue the voyage – the real one, the poetic one, Ulysses etc. – without ever catching up to it. The voyage sends me back [*me renvoie*]. A good thing it's flourishing, in you, for instance. I can only voyage in writing, which I read. I myself only travel on paper.

Roger Laporte used to say that the adventure of writing could only take place if he stayed at his desk; that's how it is these days for me, but I have moveable desks, and I come back from my explorations with notes that allow me to continue once I am back at my writing table.

My real travels undo me, distance me, a distancing that I subject myself to without being able to transcribe it. Voyages: my captivities. I've traveled throughout India, but I've never extracted the least piece of writing from this (*L'Indiade* lives on this, but none of the millions of signs I deciphered in India show up in it). Voyaging is the opposite of my writing, which is my only voyage. My love travels for me. My untraveling is all the more notable and difficult for me as I deeply love (others') travels and travelers, be they Rimbaud or his many, often surprising, doubles, all those who travel by force or by pleasure, all the ex-pelled-iled-plorers-alted, as the cosmic voyager dimension of your writing is for me one of its most touching traits, and the writers I love, among them you, are all real travelers, even Kafka, who navigated on earth as his strength allowed. As for me, when I travel (enormously) in the world, I am lost, it's someone else.

Nonetheless, I have a passion for geography. I look at globes

(I have one), I consult atlases, I think a lot by representations of continents, displacements. In my memory, my own family forms a worldwide network of dispersion, there are Kleins and Jonases in Australia as well as in Uruguay, half the countries in the world have been the jumping-off point for one or another of the family fugitives. I always have this composed-country – the country of countries – in my head, like virtual destinies. I could have been or not been [*n'être*] born [*naître*] in so many other places. Between 1920 and 1938 seeds from Osnabrück and Trnava rained on the earth. As in *De natura rerum*.

When you travel via your writing, well then, I travel.

Tokyo? Where I've been, where I'm going back to in September, if I read you there, then I'm with you there.

There is also a way – yours – of making incantations of places which then exist.

When I'm in Tokyo, I become an anthropologist, passionately I absorb the smallest details of ancient and present Japanese culture, from the taxi drivers' and gardeners' white gloves to the stone lanterns in graveyards, I absorb and I am absorbed, eaten, mute, I become printed parchment. This enlarges me, of course; it's a guarantee against any kind of circumscription, keeps the risk of French naturalization at arm's length. But it doesn't directly turn into writing.

Writing originates in books (for me).

And yet: *Tombe*, you're right, could only happen from a foreign place which had become place-(of-)book, but in disguise. The land of *Tombe*, its hells, is the country which was and still is the other, the "double" for me; it's the United States. A country productive of writing, a font of myths unlike any other, from the beginning, starting with my first "voyage," I've never been able to "arrive there" whereas it is familiar and friendly to me. That's where, every single time, I have a brush with what I call madness. I am – lost – there as if at home, "chez moi." The most threatening for me, the most

49

attractive, the least convertible, the most dis-similar. There I am in exile absolutely. I see myself double, like Manhattan's Twin Towers.

Next to Tombe, *in which one feels this desire for the novel (including in the recurrence of the characters),* Neutre *is a mixture or composite of essay and fiction, including psychoanalysis, especially Freud and Lacan, it seems to me (*Portrait of Dora *is contemporaneous with the theater of these books); then* Angst *in 1977 re-opens windows onto the interior, onto the "biographical accidents" which come back in the more recent books, heralding* Le Jour où je n'étais pas là, *published last year.*

Freud yes: as I always say *for fun*[15] is my nuncle.[16] I like him as if he were Dostoevsky's lucid moments. Immense, marvelous, admirable, descended from the caverns, grottos, abysses, and all this without the help of poetry! It's unique. Shakespeare without the shield of metaphor, a real hero. However, for me as far as the writing is concerned Lacan = zero. I knew him well, we were friends, and I believe in a respectful, sure, faithful manner. Furthermore he was an enthusiastic and mystified reader of what I was doing. Generous and modest.

As a kind of game, I had fun grafting his character and signifiers into some of my texts, a humorous wink at a Parisian scene from which I've always kept my distance.

I've conversed with Freud often. He lived next door to Kafka, really. My grandfather was from the suburbs between them (Vienna–Prague–Trnava).

---

[15] In English in the original French text.
[16] [HC's footnote in the original French text.] My nuncle, hence my non-uncle. But also my *nuncle*, the *nuncle* of King Lear, the King himself, an old fool readopted by the fools, the not-fools, Edgar the false-fool and the superwise Fool, who calls him *nuncle*. My nuncle also brings along with him the mysterious world where madness and wisdom are twins.

Lacan: a Frenchman. Like Bataille. I liked him a lot and we had whopping arguments.

Neutre is the most cryptic, slippery, terrified book. I wanted to get close to a crater and I was recoiling with fear.

You'll find there the first aborted portrait of the botched child, the one who has/is a wrong letter (note the strangeness of chromosomal notation: we are letters written more or less well, sometimes there's a spelling mistake). *Neutre* was the supreme effort to dig up the secret. All I did was shift it to another grave. Only last year did the words finally tunnel out into the open to bear witness to the Day I wasn't there. This could only happen – my son died in 1961 – because my son was finally done with his death, or done dying, it takes a long time to die, to die a death, you need to be silent for forty years. In the 1970s, and of course without ulterior motive or hindsight, I was, prey to horribly sur-viving recent events that surrounded me (the famous swords around Kafka's body) and put me to the question:[17] how to live and create with, and since, all this death and all these abandonments. I was learning how to be human, with the feeling of walking on hot coals without being a fakir. God was in the secret, in solitary confinement [*au secret*].

LAZARUS

Roosevelt Island–Paris, June 2001

Let's talk about yet another period, a subcontinent also marked by the beginning of your writing for the theater (the writing bifurcating at this point; we'll come back to this), and characterized by fresh

---

[17] "To put someone to the question" is to torture them, most commonly by tying their hands and suspending them from a rope.

publishing meanders: five books in three years (1975–7) appearing from three publishers: Gallimard, Le Seuil, Des femmes. Moreover, in the aftermath of Angst you call for "another kind of writing" where "love doesn't separate" (Angst, p. 284). Do you feel that here (but where to situate it, this passage?) you ventured into new territory, or a new stage, or that you went on digging and boring into the same ground?

The theater: pure chance. It never crossed my mind. Someone – Simone Benmussa, Jean-Louis Barrault's assistant at the time – tells me: "There's a play in that." "Where?" I say. "In *Portrait du soleil*." I'd seen nothing. She tells me: "Extract it from the text that hides it." Which I did. (And Lacan was dumbstruck. He kept asking me: but who the hell was your analyst? I didn't have one. I concluded, logically, that I had an inner analyst, among me, which was more than enough.)

Portrait de Dora was a great success, which seemed bizarre to me: all I'd done was make a copy of a glimmer in a text, "this play" that Simone Benmussa had glimpsed in the flow of *Portrait*. What a story!

However, and for that reason, I didn't think of continuing, I didn't take myself for a structural "dramatic author." I took myself for a theatrical stroke of luck. Chance, what's more is a very important character in my life. Chance: *l'hasard*. Lazarus [*Lazare*].

Angst, to my way of thinking, but I may be wrong, is less a new direction than an attempt to conclude: I told myself, really, that if I didn't get to the root of *Angst* (anguish), the mortal divinity that was persecuting me, I would die, I suffered too much from repeated *Angst*. So I engaged it as a battle. Of course I wasn't hoping to win, the main thing in a battle is to fight it, to free oneself, in acting, from the misery of passivity. So I didn't win, but I painted its portrait. Since then it has attacked me hundreds of times and still attacks me and I parry it with my pen. But you know all about that. You do the same thing. I "parry" the attack with the help of (or thanks to) these fabulous-stratagems which are the works of fiction. (Preparing the ground!)

A note about Lazarus, a signifier and proper noun which makes its way through *Le Troisième Corps*, through *Neutre*: Lazarus, the ressuscitable, a figure of the chance in which I only believe for the writing's sake, and "hazard," this magnificent word, a messenger of bliss and misery, make a tragic couple for me: let's add to them the lazaretto . . .

Let us say then, if you agree, that the new direction I glimpse is only traced at the end of Angst, *in that recapitulation of the ten first years of writing in the presence of death, in the future tense of the last, italicized "chapter," and in the last sentence, which calls for "another writing."*

*

Generically, what is it that happens in your writing at this point (at the midpoint, halfway through the 1970s) to make it oscillate between the different poles of novel, biography, tale [récit], essay? How and in what way is "biography" in the traditional sense inscribed in "bio-graphy" as Roger Laporte understands it: the bio of the graphy, the life of the writing rather than the writing of the life?

Here are two quotations from Roger Laporte to help us round out some of my previous questions, left incomplete or phrased too approximatively (the "generic" question and the commentary on the modalities of writing & travel):

"From the work-in-writing I expect what one usually asks of life, or I even go so far as to believe that I can, for myself, consider the events of my life as a man, or even those of the world as negligible, compared with what may happen to me when I write, with

what can only happen to me insofar as I write" (Une vie *[Paris: P.O.L., 1986], p. 255).*

And: "Some go looking for adventure in the four corners of the world, but traveling bores me; it quickly gives me a guilty conscience, insofar as I am convinced I have removed myself from the only place – my desk – where I can have adventures no less attractive but often more dramatic than many others" (p. 358).

These two nuances or modalities of the same idea (writing is an exclusive habit, and only the work of writing constitutes for the scripter a true "event" – for Proust it even becomes "the only life fully lived") seem to me important in order to think through the function of writing in the life of the person who writes, and so determine what's at stake. As for my reference to the bio *of the* graphy, *here's what I want to ask you: do you believe that your entire life – the "real life," the only one really lived, etc. – can be identified with your writing, and measured against it, rather than against its outstanding events? Or must one privilege the first at the expense of the second, both political and historical?*

The biographical, what a huge, impossible question, once again one of the psychic divinities I try to avoid, to forget, and you come along and waylay me with it again.

I'll pretend [*faire mine*] to answer. This is a mine, a land-mine.

(1) I don't know.

(2) Maybe, posthumously, I'll figure it out. What I do know (often said) is that I don't know how, can't, can't even make the attempt, to live without writing (and reading as part and parcel of writing). I've always thought myself infirm, sick, inept, and worse: devoid of courage, lacking the force incarnated in my mother-who-lives, cast out from the mystery of life-without-prothesis, of life as the end and means of the acts of living. I am forever hanging on a rope over the abyss. So,

in some way, live-write are factors, agents for one another, genitor-twins.

If I were kept from writing, I'd die.

It exhausts me, sometimes I want to die in order to stop writing, but this is a luxurious thought, without body. All the same, when I do die, I'll have deserved a good long sleep I tell myself; since even asleep it continues, writing dreaming write-dreaming. But I haven't answered the terrible question yet. Let's have a go at it. Is it "the real life"? This is a question or thought linked to its other: love, as I have always experienced it, as passion, absolute, the condition of living and remaining alive. Here I am then with these three legs, live write love, each of them the heart of hearts, holy of holies, necessary and non-sufficient condition for all the others.

N.B. In a book I said: the main character of the book is not who you think. Which applies to this vital reflection.

I am at least double, maybe three, structurally. That's fate, I've always felt this unconditional condition as an affliction, an almost shameful fatality; which I convince myself is congenital, probably genetic, physiological, I am a sutured thing, inseparably separated from that which separates me. What's more, I am always a little beside myself, accompanied, followed, withdrawn, distracted, from the start, divided from the start. The events happen to this divided-figure-of-me, they complicate it, repeat it while displacing it, but they don't seem to me to cause it; they have the force of a war; they can bomb, raze, eviscerate (I note that by "the events" I understand first and foremost the attacks, shocks, and blows of death). Life events – are there any? Not, it seems to me, if one conceives of the event as the sudden appearance of the unpredictable. My "life-events," I believe, as such, took place as the predecessors of my whole history, the fact of writing, the fact of loving, these mysteries were inaugural. I feel myself written, and that my story (secret, moreover) has been written and comes from very far. I am in the act of reading it. I have always already been written.

"Political" events are never, for me, anything other than the latest reenactments of ancient tragedies I know by heart. I throw myself into them out of a sense of moral obligation, but they have no secrets for me: I've already been through, read, unmasked whatever is at stake a thousand times, which doesn't keep my sense of indignation from blazing up again; still, this is a mere bump in the road, in no way comparable to the secrets of writing-loving: what preoccupies me is the unceasing struggle of the forces of death within me and mine, and to lump all this together in one huge word, I have never worked (nor did Montaigne) on anything other than the mysteries of auto-immunity. [*L'*]auto-immunity. Lotto-immunity. A word, a phenomenon, which began to interrogate my texts when I wrote *La Ville parjure*, a play on the contaminated-blood tragedy (1992–3). And which acquired, under the powerful impulse of Derrida's thinking (*cf. Foi et Savoir*, and *all* the texts after it), an extraordinarily profound amplitude and resonance. Why does *I* open the door to the destruction of me? How to not do this? See the Kafka short story in which I often used to recognize myself: "The Knock at the Manor Gate."

So this question lays its shadow over the impossibility of me not writing. I write at the cost of living the cost. Don't ask me to choose. I fear seeing myself choose: writing. This is why a powerful interdiction looms over "writing": I can't write without feeling I am wronging all the people to whom I owe my life, and the time, to write. Writing is given me: not just by writing, the language, the vast literary parentage the dead who continue in words; but by "mine" given to me and who give to me and to whom I give less than I could because I steal from them the time to write. It's endless.

Yes "realife" will have been the *working*. But not the only truly lived: the truly (*vrai-ment* [true-lies]) highest kind of living has all the same always been love but love only takes place at the expense of a struggle of the world against me. If I didn't come to my aid in writing I couldn't bear up under the harshness of the fight.

P.S. I don't remember *Souffles* at all.

EXPIRE

Roosevelt Island–Arcachon–Roscoff, August 2001

Political events and actors are present, especially in recent years: with Mandela, for instance, the events of the "outside" world enter the text. A political reading of the work is possible, such as Françoise Rossum-Guyon's. You say you have no memory of Souffles; *it is, as it happens, one of the books, like* Prométhéa, *eight years later, that is pregnant with love, with relationships and physical proximity, with passion, the whole body alive, breathing. As its title in part indicates, it is a text written on the breath that inhabits love, the body traversed by breaths.*

There too, when you read my book of madness (*Manhattan*), you will see what "I experience" (in the English sense of the word) of life, for, to, in literature. The political has persecuted me from the outset: I am three years old and the stage is already fully political and raging with war. As a matter of fact, I believe that I must have used books in emergencies to arrange flights (to be understood as all the kinds of flight): my entire life as always in history is a story of the tensions between the bombardments from the outside and the unlivable within.

With *Manne*, transferring my own fears onto other figures was also a way to try to forget the uproar within: get thee

57

hence, demons! (Theater is the same, one makes believe that the characters aren't me; it's half-true.)

Souffles: no memory at all. Except globally: I remember it as a book of desire, of relentlessness, of hunger, of crying out – yes. But the pages, the organs, nothing. And since all these books are each and every time animated by the Breaths that death (one or another death) has cut off, I don't want to go back to them.

Basically, the fact that enraged, insatiable desire throws itself onto the paper is probably because of one's presentiment that it will lead to an expiration.

WRITE IN TONGUES

New York, September 8, 2001

One other, and some other, languages people your books. In Les Commencements *you write that you spoke a third language, English, along with your two "mother" tongues, German and French, with your mother: does this mean that you hesitated between these three languages before deciding in and with which of them to write? The problem is vaster: it concerns your relationship with the "foreign mother," as Racine says, and to "the other" language (Bernhard, Lispector, Joyce, whom you've read in their respective tongues, come to mind). How did you decide about your relationship to the mother-tongue? The essential question of which language to choose is already present in the first books, and later it will often be evoked, convoked.*

I've never hesitated about the choice of a language, it's as if I wrote in the French-boat while rowing with my two second languages, English and German. English was (reasonably) held to be desirable by my mother, who sent me off alone to England at the age of thirteen. You have to picture the trip: Algiers–Marseilles, stop, Marseilles–Paris Paris–Dieppe Dieppe–Newhaven Newhaven–London. Alone. Without the least apprehension. I threw myself at English as at a substitute mother. I was proud to conquer it, expression after expression. But the country (in 1950 still bombed and ruined)! My nose remembers the smell of the privet, for an Algerian a completely foreign smell. I have loved languages with the whole of my tongue, always. I read in the language. Learned to read Brazilian for Lispector. I read of course in German, I weave the threads. Above all I seek to perceive the meticulous work, the craft of the art, I scrutinize the body of a text as a lover scrutinizes the body of her lover, each fold, mark, line. I never doze off over or by a text. I detect. I can write in English, but I only venture to do so briefly because I don't want the slightest diminishment. In French though my factories are old and I have great confidence in their secular resources. But still today I love my fiancée English, I could have become English, I am moved by and curious about this language.

To simplify, and run the risk of being wrong – but such are the rules of the game – I offer up the following hypothesis: it seems obvious that your work traverses – but swimming against the stream – the evolution of sensibility, tied to the perception of things in a context that one may already call "historical," a context detectable both in your writing and in its reception; even if you didn't belong to any of these movements, these periods more or less marked by structuralism, Tel Quel, *feminism, and what one now calls "writing the intimate." However, today, rereading your books – this for me is one of the striking things about rereading you because I wasn't conscious of this when they first came out – one realizes that writing the intimate, the body-presence, the "biographic" has always been present in your work. In* Souffles, *which I experienced for the first time twenty-six years after its publication, they are there.*

And the biographical as well, in Portrait du soleil, Tombe, *etc.: for example, with the presence of* Ève *and of* Georges, *who thanks to their emblematic names could pass, be perceived at the time, as archetypes, mythological characters (Georges and the dragon, Ève the foundational, the nourisher, etc.). Have you always covered your tracks? And if not, how did this transition between the emblematic and the intimate as such come about? In the 1970s, you were going against the current of structuralist formalism, of absolute, englobing "textuality," from which the author was excluded; already you sought to displace the biographical, situating it on the terrain of the emblematic.*

The successive periods you speak of are foreign to me: I have never belonged to any kind of circle of influence (party, genre – even gender, etc.). My impression is that from my first texts I have ceaselessly, from book to book, sought the form adequate to the themes of the coming book, whose cause was always a collision between me and the world. I've never been "in the swim" or against it, for my own direction was too strong to be swayed. What I have more than once thought is that being elsewhere I was always in a place-time without limits and without reference to the actual. My companions have always been simultaneously Kleist Shakespeare the Bible Montaigne Derrida. Nonetheless, when the scene, when events morally forced me (for example 1975 – the publishing house Des femmes), I emphasized certain aspects, out of a feeling of solidarity I enlarged them, or adopted themes that I had already gone beyond. I consider that *Le Troisième Corps* was way ahead of the regressive considerations and arguments around sexual difference. And while I resigned myself to putting on the brakes, it always annoyed me to have to act less shrewd than I was.

Yes, Ève, Georges, all the heroes of my house, a realm and a well of myths, all have always been at work in my work. I didn't plan this: I took note of the *figures* around me, always already figures and transpositions. When my mother Ève Cixous née Klein opens the door, "Eve," a legendary and textual apparition, always steps in. My father Georges was eternally, in my eyes, living or dead, alive as a survivor, always already a character from another world, the world of languages and metamorphoses, a little like a horse a bird a god a plant a knight, I didn't even have to transpose him, I saw him as gigantic, unbounded, not my mother, who has always been the concrete, marvelously limited, the wonder of her spade-like hands, both feet firmly on the ground.

N.B. I continue to think that the author, as concept of mastery, of unity of enunciation, etc., is meaningless. "The author" is one of the many co-tenants of my mental bedchamber.

The emphasis on the signifiers, on the radiations that emanate from proper nouns in particular, and then from all signifiers when we pay attention to their sounds, let's say the game, the work, the alchemy, let's say the hypersensibility, mine, to the innumerable stirrings of the Text organism, the shimmers, the calls, all these interundergroundtextualities, have always been on the qui-vive and so I have always lived-written *in* displacements, *the* displacement, the biographical always displaced displacing (changing as Rousseau would say, inchanging enchanting [*en change . . . enchangé, enchanté*]). I haven't gone looking for them, haven't done this on purpose. I add that the a-human ideology, machine etc., has always struck me as the game of an obsessive little boy and hasn't interested me for a second. I am of the Montaigne family; it's the human being his dreams and his anxieties that count for me; hence me as you.

Allow me to insert a peerless Blanchot quotation here, one that comes as it happens from the text called Après-coup *and coincides*

with what you were saying about the author, how the concept makes
no sense for you as "concept of mastery, of unity of enunciation":
". . . before the work, the writer doesn't yet exist; after the work, he
doesn't subsist: one might as well call his existence questionable, yet
we call him 'author'!"

This is cruelly exact.

What I was also trying to say is that the reference to reality is
different when you speak of Ève in the books from the 1970s and
when you say, for example, in the preface [prière d'insérer] to
Osnabrück: *"How can one write on one's living mother?" naming*
her, including her family name; there the reader understands,
knows that Éve Cixous is the mother of Hélène Cixous.

About Blanchot: just as the "prophet" before the event
doesn't exist yet; after the event he's terrified not to have had
any idea of what was coming.

About Ève 1 and Ève 2: you also need to imagine a sort of
"story of Ève" in my texts, the analysis of its Èvolution: she
changes value, function, she is more and more alive and thus
elusive, she is deposited, depositable, the reader knows that
she is "the mother of H.C.," but she doesn't know it, or rather
she knows it in her way, in her own other way, she is more
and more astonishing, a natural phenomenon. "The author"
tries to conjure her up, in every sense of the word: evoke,
exorcize, lay siege to her.

And she is also, as the end nears, more and more my mother,
I cling to her and I cling all the more as time threatens, and as
I carry her, make her speak, transfigure her, she becomes my
child. "I" live on her. I am her, I dog her every step.

We were speaking of expiration. The attention to this traverses
the whole work – and no doubt any true work. "The risk is always

62

of dying. I'm not afraid. I'm afraid to write on a too low flame. But I don't want to die, either, from burning before having written the fire all the fire" (Beethoven à jamais*). Your work seems founded upon this statement that it puts to work* in practice. *The practice of writing does produce its own economy, it regulates itself, to keep the author from burning alive, Icarus once and for all.*

FAUSTES

We're arriving on the shores of Révolutions pour plus d'un Faust *(1975) and* La *(1976), two important and phenomenal books for all they contain and imply. But first, on the periphery of these books, their editorial destiny, which constitutes, as we have already said, another striking aspect of your itinerary: why did you stay with Le Seuil, then, around this time, go to Gallimard, when* Des femmes *had been publishing you ever since* Souffles *and when two other books,* Portrait de Dora *and* Partie, *were due out there?*

As far as their editorial destiny goes, the itinerary is as follows: I was with Le Seuil. *No comment.*[18] A situation I don't wish to discuss: you have the honorable publishing house; and then in the wings, corridors, staircases, palace plots, such as exist everywhere in large firms whose head, a respectable person in this case, delegates power to ten sub-heads.

Whereupon Antoinette Fouque, whom I know not at all, calls me, asks me for a text. She founded Des femmes. I meet her. I am very impressed by her drive, her political and analytical acuity, her creativity, her generosity. I am delighted to give her *Souffles*. But I hadn't understood, I confess, hadn't foreseen the perspective of a radical militant commitment. So, without thinking about the political or editorial

---

[18] In English in the original.

63

consequences, soon after this I give *La* to Gallimard. These various gestures also speak of course to my withdrawal from Le Seuil – which I never had the feeling of being attached to or identified with. At the time I didn't calculate, I went. Seeing Antoinette Fouque's emotion and listening to her talk about her surprise and chagrin at seeing me go back to the large, major (and of course, as one used to put it, "phallocratic") publishers I became aware of the connection between the gestures of social inscription and the fact that the literary work, which for me existed in the sublime, was grounded in a political and analytical rationality, and more specifically in the realm of gender.

I hadn't chosen sides. So I chose (party and parcel for the first and last time of my life). Despite my philosophicoliterary reticence about the dichotomy, the opposition, etc., and my refusal to set myself up against the father brother son figures, who for me in any case were and always had been unstable and undecidable (my father was a stork and not a phallocrat, my brother was the same dog as me), I had been without any hesitation on the side of, or beside, women since early childhood, thanks to my midwife-mother, thanks to my Algerian then Parisian experience. Since there was a struggle, I took part, although, I must emphasize, very belatedly. Antoinette Fouque started it all in 1968. Only in 1975 or even in 1976 did I throw in my lot with this world.

Here we are already in the middle of the history of the women's movement, which cuts through the 1970s. We have a Faust *(written in 1971, but only published in 1975) and then* La *(1976) – a revolution between the two?*

All that seems so far away! (It's remarkable that other books, even if they are older, are closer or more familiar to me, as if the Fausts were from a country (become) foreign.)

Your reflection clarifies things for me: you are surely correct, even if, living through it, I was not unaware of it, between a *Faust* and a *La* there must have been a revolution, to put it mildly. (One long ago day, I no longer know when, I wrote a text called "Rêvolution," playing on *rêve*, the French word for dream, a text which was even, I believe, published in *Le Monde*.) Not a revolution, nor the revolution, but rather: revolutions. Surely the "la" was increasing in importance.

That said, Faust as dreamer and lover in the second part of *Faust* moved me tremendously, the father of the phial – Euphorion; it's poignant and surprisingly modern.

In La *there's at least a three-way polysemy, if we can twist the neck of the spelling a little:* là, *meaning "there," + the two meanings of* la *(the feminine article, the musical note, the "A" that sets the tone). What else in this title? This book of the dead (Egyptian and maybe Tibetan too) which turns up in the middle of the women's liberation movement, without much resembling it? A revolution for a new kind of Faust? The female version – Fauste?*

La (yes, you're right three times *la*) precedes my discovery of the world of women's lib (which is why it went elsewhere). It is indeed steeped in the admirable texts of the Egyptian and Tibetan Books of the Dead, always close to me: I went down their paths very early, probably in the same way as in my imagination I took the path of my dead father, I felt, feel at home there. Add to this echoes of significances from Blanchot and Derrida (all the, for me, musical themes of *pas, là, ja* [not/ step, there, yes]). And to ground it all [*pour sol*] my delight in Freud's wonderful ravings in *The Interpretation of Dreams*, the basso continuo of the "Key to Dreams." At the time the ana- lytical phallic was getting on my nerves, we were in a period of much more heavy-handed phallogocentric emphases than now and all centers of thought, Paris in particular, were

65

heavily masculine and devoid of imagination, with the exception of the off-stage Derridean.

P.S. Lovely, the idea of feminizing Faust. Would I have played with the idea myself? I think Faust incarnates the mourning, the specifically masculine, as I see it, melancholy of "I don't want to grow old." Women, the ones with a heart, grow old magnificently (I know some) like Proust's grandmother – as long as they're not in thrall to the male gaze.

N.B. This *vieillir* is not the English verb "to age," it's an exploration. *La* is ageless.

Clairvoy

New York–Paris, September 20–5, 2001,
October 11–14, 2001

So far I've resisted the temptation to come directly to the present, to zigzag between past and present, I've refused to do so; however, it strikes me that today, especially since you've allowed me to read the manuscript of your New York book, written this summer, 2001, just before the catastrophe and erasure of an entire New York neighborhood, we can't not speak of events that have affected us so powerfully – it seems to me that at the very least I can't go on asking you about the beginning of your career without opening a parenthesis here and making a detour via your most recent book, not yet, as we speak, published.[19]

I return to my questioning, to this, shall we say, gentle inquisition, after the summer's rather long interruption – first the battle of Arcachon for you, that of Roscoff for me,[20] *then this horror upon*

---

[19] Published in 2002, as *Manhattan. Lettres de la préhistoire.*

[20] Arcachon, near Bordeaux, where Cixous summers. *La Bataille d'Arcachon* (1986) is also the title of one of her books. Roscoff is a village

my return to New York, of the Twin Towers' collapse in the heart of Manhattan. I am struck by your powers of divination: the book you wrote this summer, called for the moment Le Récit, *reads like a premonition, a double for the symbolic towers.*

Leafing through the past few months of your interview, I see that I haven't stopped talking about the United States, New York, the Towers, *seeing double.*

Then on the phone I mentioned my post-tower, post-*twin* anxiety to you – the small fear at the sensation of having been premonitory. But, I tell myself, one *never knows* that one is premonitory *before*, it's *afterwards* that one becomes aware of the "presentiment," which should be called pre-presentiment, and that one feels fear at having crossed the abyss unawares.

October 17–18, 2001

This detour also lets us address and try to define your writing method at this time. What about this sort of prescience, premonition, or clairvoyance that makes you anticipate events?

I'm wondering why I was so quick to send you "this summer's book," which has only a provisional title as yet (all my books are like this: born under a name, shall we say a pet name, a "nickname," a false one, which is perhaps the true one? – and eventually I have to give them their "proper name," register them with the authorities, which I am totally incapable of doing, with the result that I wait for "God" to do it, always *in extremis*) – a provisional title, therefore; for the time being it seems to be *Le Récit* – the eternal impossible – I wonder why – and I answer:

---

in Brittany where Frédéric-Yves Jeannet had gone that year to write – to engage in the "battle of writing."

(1) Probably it's so that it becomes *a book* at the first opportunity: that is, to free myself from its presence within me, which brings with it certain worries; maybe it even made me ill, maybe it awoke the pneumonia in me, who knows, I'd begun it, framed it, shored it up in April, at top speed, running away from it as fast as I could, all that I spoke and thought was lung, maybe it caught up with me – in any case I was dumbfounded when I came down with acute pneumonia on June 28, as I was setting off for Arcachon to reunite with "it," the book, The Tale [*Le Récit*], the madness. And I wrote in July–August possessed by this physical and mental demon and spurred on or slowed down by a relentless fever.

(2) The eyes of my imagination were turned, once again, but this time explicitly, toward New York, hence from afar, I saw you there and I asked you to send me the *maps*[21] which I used every day, with a magnifying glass, to help me write, even if I transposed, displaced, refigured.

It's strange, but in bolstering myself with so much reality I was able to dream. And then, my old panicky terror at New York, which goes back to 1963, still present, only becomes bearable if I can conjure up a safety hatch, if need be, in case of mental breakage, in the person of someone who wishes me well.

Only the extreme ever happens to me in New York. And only the extreme happens there. I never touch down without trembling and without wondering if I will find myself there, if I will find it there, if the temples are still standing or ruined – tower or cave or temples. It's foundational: once, long ago, I began to need to write toward New York. This is why I had no other title than this modest, this insignificant, this all-powerful *Le Récit*.

---

[21] In English in the original French text, and in *Manhattan*.

So I also sent it to you (1) to get it away from me; (2) to bring it closer; (3) obviously, to exorcize it. It is overcharged with secret powers.

Just imagine that, even to answer you, I who usually sit down to do so easily and with pleasure, when it came to that book, I dragged my feet and fled as I have every time for decades.

Today (it is 3:30 p.m. on Wednesday) I've just taken my mother to Roissy airport, off to Manchester to see her sister, she departed gaily and bravely, leaning on an umbrella whereas I was sick with worry for her, for her sprightly ninety-one years of age. Then I brought home this picture of undauntedness coming up to the hurdle, and no excuse to balk except that I have a headache – for *everything* haunts me, Roissy airplanes headlines worry for those I love worry for the peoples trying not to die – all this horribly *concrete* in my dreams.

So this sort of "prescience, premonition" as you call it, which is supposed to make me "anticipate events." Well I tell myself that, there's no science involved. That's what's frightening. I *know nothing* – when I analyze politically (which I do endlessly) it's clear, objective, I think sensible, this is another matter. What scares me is the "*self-fulfilling*" – if I can call it so – power of nightmares. As if what happens at night and which is incredibly complex rich comic tragic *usurped* the place of day. Or as if I constantly received proof that all is written, that there are gods, demons, call it structure or DNA or combinations of thousands of notions and drives that elaborate, engender destinies, and that I, like a medium or a person with a mental or nervous illness, received telegraphically, very fast, information that has nothing magical or inexplicable about it, except that I myself don't know the explanation.

Besides, I have no presentiment. I recognize what happens to me for having dreamt it the night before.

69

(Interruption – the visit of my friend Alia Mamdouh, a writer exiled from Baghdad: "change" of viewpoint – she fears the United States, suffers for the Iraq she flees. Our time: mirrors full of fears, we reflect one another to infinity, and no one recognizes anything but Fear.)

Paris, October 18, 2001

Thursday – I pick this up again this morning. One thought, about New York: I think: poor New York, as if I could bend over the city as over a cradle! Yet, and therefore forever, I experience her (she is feminine for me, another mystery, but this is no doubt the femininity of the masculine, a phallic fragility) as: New York – eternally – bombed and bombarding me. So many phantasms seek shelter in her shell. And after all if she really was bombed, *she*, above all, it's because she was desired, desirable.

I have no premonitions. (But – for the theatrical work – Ariane Mnouchkine and I repeated again and again that it was strangely *prophetic*. Obviously the prophet is (1) alerted by messages that are not necessarily verbal, he is a reader of signs, a detector of creaks; (2) but there is also *the repetition*, a fatality that we humans have difficulty integrating and thinking about, the return, sometimes decades later, sometimes centuries later, of events that seem to be happening for the first time but which have already occurred.)

About *Le Récit*, the events happened forty years ago and didn't – don't – stop happening; so maybe I was hearing creaks in the politicoterrestial crust.

Unfinish the Hi/story

Roosevelt Island–New York, October 1, 2001
Fax, November 3, 2001

Prophetic, you say, of the theater work. It also has an immediate political side: La Ville parjure *wrestles with AIDS, the contaminated-blood scandal. Similarly, the fictional text,* Manne aux Mandelstams aux Mandelas, *is rooted in the present and takes an option on the future "the unfinished hi/story," would you agree? I'm thinking especially of those characters based on persons who are alive at the time you are writing: Winnie and Nelson Mandela, whose marriage was subsequently dissolved. As well as Norodom Sihanouk, with whom you corresponded, Zhou Enlai, Alexis Kossyguine. So here you side with the living.*

It could be "the immediate political side": a whiff of current events. However, I don't think I was ever "current," I never observed, thought of the news as happening in the present, rather I was sensitive to a present, a here-and-now whose aura of having plural tenses, past, future, pastfuture, etc., attracts me: in other words, only the scene or event, as carrier, transporter of other analogous scenes, only therefore the metaphors speak to me. The Mandelas were only interesting as Mandelstams, the desert of the veld as Siberian snow; Tristan and Isolde or Siegfried-Kriemhild: it's always the same couple, the man in danger watched over by his lover (and maybe it's my father dying, unawares, my mother a bit absent-minded?).

I could, but really don't want to, point to an analytical, political, and autobiographical mythology-typology. But this would be to formalize and schematize something that I experience "with my eyes shut."

To come back to *characters who are living people*, in my

creative life it's an enormous adventure, this *daring* [*oser*] to transpose [*transp'oser*] people who are living – but who are already bigger-than-life, because already, in their lifetimes, *characters*. I've only ever done it in fear and trembling, and cheating with my own trembling. For the Mandelas the question of the judgment of Winnie came along, like a response to my audacity. As we know she is forever accused on one side, and on the other adulated by the little people. For me, the Winnie of the book has an undeniable truth-reality, she was the Winnie of Nelson in chains – as in the life as in the tragedy. Lives are composed of several lives and several deaths. The succession, the replacement, the alteration, it all needs to be worked out.

But, once again, I was never a realist: the *Mandelas* were an African version of Shelley's *Prometheus Unbound* (a stupefying, strange, projective, austere text. The lover is called Asia. Allegory).

"The unfinished hi/story" is almost redundant, don't you think? Hi/stories are always unfinished. One tells them to try to *finish* them (off) in every sense of the term. Pin them down. And telling stirs up. And a little while later, when the hi/story has apparently been counted and recounted, time comes along and undoes it and tells it differently. Hi/story is never dead, and yet "telling" is storing, burying, exhuming but at the same time closing again. That's why I like only the unfinishable, the stories that escape us. That decamp. Winnie – still at loose!

Sihanouk: such a long story. When I was writing it, Ariane and I were in perfect agreement that once the play was "finished," I would disguise all the names. I should have known this wouldn't happen, since to write I needed the real names. To analyze this: to get close to the secrets I needed to call them by their proper names. As if the name had been/was part of the soul. Sihanouk – I only met him *after* having written: not too much reality = more "truth": that is, truth as invention-of-the-truth.

Everything I write is *invented*, at a minimum translated. Translated from French, from memory, from witnesses' accounts, of the *so-called*[22] reality. It's like Proust's strange "I," who is the author's puppet, his I and his not-I.

October 18, 2001

What I also meant by "your writing method at this time" in my fax earlier, was this: the writing of a book, over the summer, in your annual battle of Arcachon, how does it absorb what's going on in the outside world, how does it stay "in touch" when, precisely, you must cut yourself off from the world, withdraw from it in order to write?

I don't know how writing a book (a vast question and beyond me) is linked to "what's going on in the outside world." What I do know – this is very superficial – is that it has a tidal rhythm. It comes. And I come to it. Ritually. Organically. I don't, it appears, prepare myself except spiritually and physically. Nonetheless, since it *comes*, and comes on time, *it* is prepared, somewhere far from my conscious awareness, but all year long; it nourishes itself on the world – on my seminar research,[23] on my emotional archives. But, as I say in *Le Récit*, I never have any idea, either of the theme or of the object, I have only a *law*: head for whatever is the most frightening. To that which I cannot and do not want to write face-to-face.

"Cutting myself off from the world" as noise, yes, this is necessary – but I hold onto the furor.

---

[22] In English in the original French text.
[23] Hélène Cixous conducts a seminar, open to the public, in Paris, during the academic year.

Furthermore, current events rarely appear to me as "current." I am more accustomed to endlessly deciphering the depths, the very ancient dramas under "the news" (I ought to say "the newsbiz") – all these things are the metaphors of our passions; I conjure up the state of the Trojans when their New York was gutted. We are the same modernized primitives. Anguishes are ageless. Which is also why I'd *already* written *Le Récit*, but from a distance, askance, with shield and disguise, in *Tombe*, distancing it, making a travesty of it, fleeing it. Similarly, haltingly, I'd written *Le Jour où je n'étais pas là* in *Neutre*. Which shows that it has taken me thirty years to drag *the Thing* from the mud and meconium. Thirty years is a long time and it's nothing.

Let's touch on your very particular writing process or protocol at present (a present that doesn't necessarily coincide with the present tense): in a single breath, in a trance, keeping in mind the whole cathedral, you said on the phone, keeping the construction of the book in your head during the entire course of its writing. Do you always write the whole book this way? Have all your books appeared to you, have they all been written like this?

As far as time, the duration goes – as I told you, I *cannot write* except uninterruptedly: it's impossible: hence in a trance. Otherwise I'd be sidetracked by resistances and fears. I only write red-hot, in convulsions, it's highly physical, it's exhausting, it's a gallop, I write ten hours straight, I collapse, but with paper, I don't stop, when I am too tired, I take notes in the evening, at night so as to start fresh, as if heading off to battle, at daybreak, and I do this for two months. During this time I keep in mind the book's *landscape* or *land*, its mental map, its armies, its armoires, scraps of sentences, images, dreams, its passages. But not its "whole," not its composition. This I don't know, I discover.

For the same reason, as soon as the "book" "ends" it withdraws like a tide, and I no longer remember anything.

During this time, being "with-book" as *with child*,[24] being nothing but the book, I can't interrupt myself, not at all, which is why I maintain absolute solitude, accompanied without fault by my mother, who takes care of everything, shopping, cooking, etc., and whom I make part of the writing so she won't be excluded or foreign to it and break the spell. In short I "sleep" two months.

JUST BEFORE THE PAPER

New York, October 20
Sunday, Montsouris, pouring rain, October 21, 2001

An examination of certain manuscripts that you have deposited in the Bibliothèque nationale shows that they have very few corrections – as in the faxes in which you respond to mine – and that their flow is regular, almost without "pentimenti": second thoughts or crossings-out. How do you do this, how are you able to accomplish this: do the sentences come into being quickly, haltingly; or do you not write them down until they are ready, like newborns delivered with their eyes open and all their hair, or children whose first words are complete sentences? The regular calligraphy of your manuscripts doesn't in any case bring to mind precipitation or trance-states. Do you copy them out? In my case the formulation is so slow and laborious, forever provisional and subject to infinite, successive modifications, that I would like to understand your process: one tells oneself reading you that your sentences couldn't be changed, that there's nothing to cut or to add. If, in addition, that's how they come into the world, it's astonishing.

---

[24] In English in the original French text.

75

Reading your beautiful question I noticed that I was about to feel guilty for not having second thoughts! Then you write: "How do you do this?" As a matter of fact *I* don't. *They* do.

To say something conscious I have to break down a door, a partition, behind which they, the sentences, are made. In the wings? But what *can* I say? Yes, they are born, they come to me, I always have the feeling they are like the angel behind Saint Matthew, Rembrandt's painting, those who dictate to me sit on my shoulder, in back of me, they slide down my arm, right to my fingertips. Since this is *physical*, albeit angelical, I can't use any machine, I take the dictation down, fast. You evoke talking newborns, it couldn't be more similar: I myself often dream of talking babies, who fill me[25] with astonishment. What occurs: there is a precise speed – slow speed or speedy slowness – of dictation which means that as I note what is being dictated I have *the time* "to record" what is surging up, to spot the games the moment they occur (for example: in *bouchent bouche*, the homonymy happens all by itself but, in a tenth of a second, I am sensitive to it, and someone inside me, on my left, in the eleventh of a second, re-injects into the nervous-cerebral circuits a system of signifiers, promptly relayed). Let's say that inside me several beings, worker-secretary-scribes, simultaneously pass the word – the words.

Anyway I, or at least this writing machine within me, can only act if I am acted upon, set in action, propelled, by passion. It's like a spark: I think and I am; something flashes, thinks, inside me before any thought, and I, fingers curled around my pen, I am that which always presents itself as message-vision-of-thought. Since there is this infinitesimal time lapse, half a second or a second, I have time to pause so the

---

[25] In French, *qui m'en bouchent un coin*; allowing the play on words with *bouchent* ("fill, plug") and *bouche* ("mouth").

right word comes along, the one that's indispensable in this place. This word, strangely, I "sense" it before I pronounce it, I feel it get up, come. Arrive to me.

I re-copy very little: at least for most of the text. Very often I spin my (thinking) wheels and therefore I throw down on paper one, two, three, four initial versions, because my thinking is a little foggy. Or maybe it's so extremely complicated that I don't know which end of the skein to grab. But it's always at the level – a mine landing – of the thought that I can find myself hobbled. The phrasing is a loyal helper – once the thought has found its direction. Clearly your practice and your art are the opposite of mine. I don't do the revising you do with your texts. *But*: I am absolutely convinced that this work of revision, which, in your work, happens once you are on the terrain of the paper, happens similarly *in me*, *before* the paper. I see myself, sense myself, having drafted at full speed in the mental desk in back of my brow, and *then* extracting a version already more or less satisfactory before committing it to paper.

How do you manage to circumscribe in time the trance *process that you mention, and which one feels very strongly in some of your opening chapters* (Les Rêveries de la femme sauvage, *for one)? It must be exhausting; you prepare yourself like an athlete for a race, you've told me, but don't you suffer from having to repress this urge during the entire rest of the year, then to break off again when summer ends?*

I used not to be able to master this urge. I never stopped being-en-route – being-en-route to being at the point of – I took notes everywhere and anywhere – fear of losing something, of letting something go by and especially the primitive fear of "stopping" the flow, drying it up, of losing all the writing if I didn't keep going.

Then came *reality*: I couldn't, without wearing myself out intellectually, be going all the time from the world of infinite liberty to the social, professional, regulated world. The constant distraction unbalanced me. Gradually therefore I apprenticed myself to another economy. In the manner of yogis. As a matter of fact, I have the same approach to food: I manage, I order my meals with the writing in mind. I never eat lunch, for the writing wants to stay the course for eight or ten hours straight, without a break.

To tell the truth, all I did was to choose, between two kinds of ill-being or suffering, the one least unlivable for me. It's as if I asked myself, me the child wild to write, to be patient, promising in exchange to grant all the child's wishes when the time came. Besides, I am a being capable of being patient and waiting, not spontaneously, but by dint of habit and exercitation.

On the other hand come summer I become virulently intolerant, no restraint, I can be subject to flashes of anger, of hate if anything or anyone at all puts obstacles in my path. But this is out of the question: I am for the writing and only the writing. Only death can turn me aside.

During the year, waiting patiently, I am not of course completely drained. But the water level remains deep underground and held in reserve. This said, a little writing trickles out in the form of accounts of my dreams, for instance – hence some dozens of pages, notations.

THE FORGETREAD

New York, October 14–15, 2001

I am surprised (is this significant?) to see that the style – I'd even go so far as to say the syntax – of Faust (Révolutions pour plus d'un Faust, *completed in 1971) differs considerably (with all its mythology, references, and the dialogues that seem to prefigure the theater, in which you only officially became involved, it seems to me, in 1975 with* Portrait of Dora; *I can't speak about* La Pupille, *I can't find a copy) from that of books such as* Neutre *or* Le Troisième Corps, *written at the same time.*

Does each book imply a kind of rejection of the one before, even very recent; is each one a search for and immersion in another thing, which calls for its own syntax; an attempt to find in your language (which I call Cixaldian, to rhyme with "Rimbaldian") another language, or more exactly another register and other modes of writing, which hence each time leave different traces?

All this to say that I am trying to define this strange phenomenon you speak of: certain older books are, and remain, closer to you than Faust *and* La. *A phenomenon that I understand, which I experience in my own work, but which I would like to hear you talk about; how does this come about, where, this closeness or distance? What about other texts we could juxtapose with* Faust *and* La, *after the 1975 turning point: that is, when your "commitment" to the Des femmes is becoming stronger:* Partie, Préparatifs de noces, Vivre l'orange, Ananké? *(We've already spoken a little of* Angst.*) Are these books still close to you? Were they trying to unearth a new direction, or perhaps excavate a little more of this hole "at the bottom of which they will bury us in the end," as my friend Pascal Engel once wrote me?*

So, *Faust* (it's already closer to me for being called simply that, familiarly, by you). My memories: nebulous. More the memory of a *state of mind*:

(1) I was looking for a way, for a form, in which to account for events, political facts that distressed me, but charged with a realism that silenced me. Basically, if I'd been at the Théâtre du Soleil already I would have known what to do. For example: *La Ville parjure*, a combination of the most recent, the

most up-to-date (the tainted blood), and the most ancient (the Eumenides). *Faust* therefore is probably for want of a theater.

Was there a movement of rejection? It would seem to me to be closer to the truth to see in these mutations of genre the second thoughts, the revisions that I don't make in my sentences. I was essaying. I was writing my Essays. I was trying to surround or besiege the great world by different roads and doors. Probably I must also have been moved by a resistance to settling down, to repetition, to becoming established. I chose the route of wandering. With my paw, my feather, I was testing formal possibilities, to see where they would lead me. And then I went further.

(2) This was a period when I was politicized on a daily basis, as "naturally," if I can put it that way, as possible; from me to the world there were only a few steps, protesting was like school, one went – furthermore I went with my children as soon as they could keep up (already in 1968) – I think that at the time there was hardly any distance between literary and political sensibility; and I was looking for the pass, or the col. I found myself too lyrical, too much an explorer of intimacy, I didn't know how to make the massacred talk. *Faust* is a product of this experimental laboratory, it's a trial, an essay, but it didn't satisfy me, I was in need of characters who would be more personal. (*La Pupille*, I have no idea, there must be a copy around, I don't know where, I'm going to investigate.) *Neutre*, however stylized and distilled, is much closer to me, for in it I was dealing with motifs that for me are fundamental: destiny, hazard, chance, the missing letter. Even if it is – it was – a mask, but no more of a mask, for example, than Edgar Poe's fable-masks, which I still delight to read. On the other hand the transgressiveness of its ultramodern technique (nobody wrote like that at the time, it knocked my readership for a loop) might be compared to techniques of composing

80

contemporary music. But I myself found it to have a kind of aridity caused by my fear of *touching* the wound.

P.S. October 21, 2001: Sentences: I am crazy about sentences, I believe I've tried everything. I know their names, their ruses, their quantities, their poetics, their rhetorical resources. When they come along, it's they who choose their aspect – parataxis, nominal. It's according to their will.

Of the first three books cited above, Préparatifs de noces *is probably the one that is a hinge with the books that preceded it (I mean it still belongs with them). With* Ananké *and perhaps above all* Vivre l'orange *it seems to me that something new happens – something, furthermore, that I can't quite define, perhaps linked to the feminine, the political commitment and the art of the philosophical essay, more oriented toward the expression of a thought than toward the transmission of sensations? As for* Partie, *it is typographically wild, like* Finnegans Wake, Tristram Shandy – *a very strange book considering the rest of your work from this period, with a larger part being given over to Joycian games on, with, in the language, portmanteau words, etc. Almost diametrically opposed therefore to* Vivre l'orange.

I had a lot of fun with *Partie*, and my children did too. My son still quotes fragments. It's the Lewis Carroll side that makes him laugh. *Partie* is a book which plays on the verbal fetishization of the period's popes (my friend Lacan for one, whom I like immensely, the solemnity of whose utterances, whose linguistic inventions promptly cooled and petrified into concepts, made me laugh). That said, the characters of *Partie* were heroes after my own sense of fantasy: I borrowed a great deal from Plutarch, whose *Lives* still today are for me utterly magical. Was I leaning toward the elusiveness of the extreme text?

Probably. I also believed I was allowed to be as free I liked,

81

which retrospectively tells me how naïve I was. I believed that one could venture into writing like a painter. But this remains unacceptable. *Partie*, in any case, was not meant to produce offspring.

During this experimental phase I did some alchemical – or perhaps sporting, or hallucinatory – experiments on purpose, as if to try out the writing instrument, take the measure of its strengths and limits, and also test editorial and critical resistance: all the same people were pretty dumbfounded. I pushed the limits, deliberately, actively.

To come back to your idea of the *rejection* of one text by another: this strikes me as illuminating. I didn't think of it. But it might be true, without my knowing it. In fact, I didn't think to stay with any of those texts. Who knows if I wasn't running away from myself? And then there was also the ease with which I changed – change – writing, for the writing has such numerous voices, and my ingrained and ongoing practice of reading has always kept alive within me a chorus of extremely diverse voices, or languages – I mean languages like Shakespeare, Montaigne, Villon. . .

Préparatifs: cut off from me. I know that it resonates (-ed) with many readers, but it has drifted off, unlike *Angst*, which has come closer. In those days I sought, with genuine anxiety, "women's" texts: I told myself I couldn't go through life without the company of female peers; even if I adored Kafka I felt myself without an echo of reply, all the more so as on the politico-social-institutional scene, there were men (only), and so masculine, save Derrida, that the world could not imagine a feminine sensibility or states of mind – except Shakespeare and Kleist – but that didn't suffice (see Proust, whom I read a great deal *now*, there was no innerness save masculine, not one woman is lit up from within), and I was scared. So I began to roam the world of libraries to see if there mightn't be on the other side a door I had failed to try. That's when the work of Clarice Lispector happened to me. And not long after, Anna Akhmatova, Marina Tsvetayeva, Ingeborg Bachmann. So I was reassured, as if I had a sort of family to visit and depart from. I felt myself read and understood by friends I hadn't met, whom I would never meet.

This company of in-reality-unknowns whom I cherished would not have sufficed to nudge me into the more markedly feminine regions if I hadn't then, contemporaneously, been taken in by Antoinette Fouque's éditions Des femmes. The number of coincidences, of chances, which have come to my rescue at the right moment is remarkable. But maybe chance only awaits a sign to manifest itself? At the very moment I was losing hope of seeing a hand held out, a place. Sometimes I allow myself to think (or I fear thinking) that things always happen this way in my life: the last-minute rescue.

Something that occurred to me – about *Faust*, *Partie*, etc. – last night: the form of those texts, that embarkation for unknown continents, was probably also over-determined by my own inner state, a little disastrous, by an emotional gagging which occurred at that time. I have a tendency to forget about this, or to keep it off to one side. But those few years, maybe three, were among the years of disavowal, of inner disavowal, when the heart, so necessary to the writing, its motor, having been intimidated, becomes wordless, loses its exuberance. I was, you could say, without myself, or with a self that felt threatened and holed up in a den.

I imagine that those verbal *ex*cursions were also controlled by the necessity to keep the pen far from the damaged body.

But perhaps this reflection is a construction? What is not is the coincidence between the distant verbal expeditions and my affective exile. What makes me doubt is that exile is for me a recurrent experience. I also feel that I must have traversed a time of ethical interrogation, of the kind Stendhal speaks of: all this "me" is perhaps indecent? A thought I must have had before rejecting this as false, absurd, and most likely brought on by aggressions from the outside.

(There are always trials going on off to the side, when one writes, don't you think, coming from places of narrow-minded reading, and which still at times make one hesitate, waver. I've known many, too many, of such instances of reprobation; up until 1980–1, I was sensitive to them, then no more, not at all.)

OTHER ADDRESSES

We know that "since forever" you are on the side of Joyce, to whom you have dedicated several essays, in particular your thesis, L'Exil de Joyce ou l'art du remplacement, *which was published, as we've seen, just after* Le Prénom de Dieu, *though it was written before. After that came* Prénoms de personne, *which also shed light on Joyce. As for your relationship with other great actors of our modernity, that with Proust is more ambiguous; of him you say that there is "no innerness save masculine," and you speak harshly of him in* La: *"Refuse to be among the sick, dragging themselves around in the company of their malady [. . .], a tenant in the hotel of lost time . . .," "Mentality of a hermit crab, of grottos, of cork-lined rooms . . .," ". . . crab of the depths . . .," ". . . necrophiliac son . . .," ". . . the born-disconsolate . . .," ". . . he who believes that there is lost time is not among the living . . .," etc. (pp. 262–3). Still, elsewhere in your texts, we find sorts of indirect homages to Proust, even in the language sometimes, although it is true these are less perceptible than your Joycean detours. What today is your relationship to Proust?*

What goes on between Proust and me is a mixture of extremes. For a long time I *could not* read him, any more than I could step into a salon. Which tells you the force of his text:

the fiction gives such a strong sense of "reality" that it felt to me like a real world, but one in which I had not the least wish to linger. The social world raised my hackles, the nobility's particules, salons, mediocrities, I took it all "literally" as reality. As I abhor salons, cocktails, receptions, "high" society, whose invitations I toss out week after week.

It took me decades to arrive at a place where I could dissociate my realist antipathy from my immense admiration for the art. I read him now with great intellectual joy and I believe great respect, I know his phraseology well; but the familiarity, the feeling of deep, intimate kinship, without gnashing of teeth, that I have for Kafka, no.

Proust has been read in my seminar (by me) for years, in great depth. But I will never find there that which causes one to weep with joy, the sadness and the rightness that make one's heart ache.

Along with that, there is the writing of women: you cite Lispector, Akhmatova, Tsvetayeva, who appear in your books, critical texts, and "fiction" – but what relationship do you have, for example, with Dickinson and Woolf? (I mention them because I myself feel a closeness, not only between them, among the three of you, but with them, myself.)

Well, it's a little the same for Woolf. I admire her language, her art, the splendid power but, aside from *Orlando*, which I love, her characters bore me a little to death as if I had to spend a lifetime with them, and I find her death drive – except in *Orlando* the freed – painful. So I do her homage since I recognize – in distancing myself from it – the extreme force of her creation. All the same I never read Virginia Woolf for my pleasure.

Emily Dickinson – I feel I can't be precise about her. A little as with Melville: they are among the great whom for no good reason I have not sufficiently approached. I ask myself a lot of questions about this. At times I start to think it is a matter of bizarre climatic, geographic determinations: why do I always look first toward the east or northeast of my body-thought? Toward the north, for example, whereas I myself am from the South and the Southwest? I don't understand myself.

I think too that I need a brazier of historical experience, a horizon of events, to sense a center of political suffering, as is the case for Lispector, Akhmatova, Tsvetayeva, Bachmann. (Woolf doesn't lack this, but she comes from the same milieu as Proust, and within me there's a little Jewish girl who feels so removed from these social classes, whereas in fact I do love what moments I have been able to spend among the secular and literary velours of English manors. Yet another contradiction.)

Do you have the feeling that your work has offspring among contemporary writers? Descendants in a family tree whose roots you share? Have you descendants already? (It seems to me that you are so much "at the extreme tip," as Roger Laporte said of his studies of Blanchot and others, that it might be impossible to find people of my generation writing anything that goes quite so far.)

I am grateful to you for this question: it lets me go beyond a private shyness that keeps me from pondering the question of descendants out of a sort of modesty *and* a secret astonishment as well. Let me explain: yes, for the last few years the possibility of such a thing has arisen, coming initially from my "descendants" themselves, who have told me about *their* feeling. In the case of literary affiliation, the movement is the opposite of that proper to genealogical affiliation. The "descendants" adopt their antecedents. As a result, the "descendants" who come along as marvelous bearers of a

86

future don't in appearance resemble the person to whom they are linked. What there is in common, and which is essential, belongs to the spiritual region of literature, to the philosophical and ethical anchorage. You, for example, a precious friend, have given me matter for thought concerning the strangeness of this link. When I began to read you, there was a deep assent, a recognition of a text previously unknown and which imposed itself as coming from a deep affiliation. I recognize a footstep. You walk, you make me think of "walking man," Giacometti biglittle I know your stride, your scansion becomes as close to me as a familiar music to which I return again and again, such an encounter and feeling of consent are rare, though they can happen. I think of this often, telling myself that my future library is already in place, I can hear the breath of works already formed, that will extend beyond my death, and for me, this is happiness, this adds life to my life. "To have children" late in life is a wonderful experience! It made Sarah laugh and thrilled Abraham. It's miraculous. One wants to be proud but one can only be humble. For one is not the cause of these marvelous "descendants," nor the condition, but only the first person, more or less, to see the great future approaching, at which one will not be present, but where one will be recollected, kept by a person in whom one is glad to be continued.

New York, December 3, 2004

As I see now, three years later, going over this text again to prepare it for publication, I needed to change subjects *without warning after these lines, which moved me. Let me add that in these elders whom I adopt I seek today neither mother nor father; rather sister & brother spirits.*

*

You were speaking of the "verbal fetishization of the period's popes," such as Lacan, but there is also a fetishization of writing: "Telquel-ism,"[26] teltextualism, the reign of textuality, etc. To the purely typographical aspect of this adventure, which Partie *represented by being printed head to tail,[27] is grafted another interrogation: is the physical aspect of the book, which one becomes conscious of in some of yours, an important preoccupation for you (illustrated in certain pages of* Tombe *and in your third* Portrait, *that of* Jacques Derrida en jeune saint juif)? Were Mallarmé, Apollinaire, or Joyce in this sense fathers (or nuncles, like Freud)? Similarly one might inquire about the proof-reading stage: do you return at this moment to the text's visuals?*

The physical side of the book: strangely I am totally *and* not in the least attached to it: I do what the book wants, I'm not in charge. *Partie* imposed itself upon me. I do note, however, that publishers are less than thrilled when one strays from the traditional format. Although Galilée (the generous Michel Delorme, that is) is, however, eager and adventurous. But basically, the text, when it is hidden, figures this in the words, hastening before the cock crows, pale, already almost effaced, shimmering and on the verge of fainting, already almost invisible – this is my preference. But sometimes the letter, the letters want to be noticed, and often I mentally underline and then I wonder if I ought to help get the message across with a typographical mark, or leave it to the reader to notice or not notice, to make this flare up or not. I always

---

[26] *Tel Quel* (1960–82) was a French literary journal and movement, whose major figures included Michel Foucault, Julia Kristeva, Philippe Sollers, and Roland Barthes.

[27] *Partie* is printed so that it can be read (to its middle) left to right or right to left.

have a fear of insisting too much. Mallarmé, Apollinaire, Joyce, no, no nuncles. I don't think (I might be wrong) I waited for them to come along. It seems to me that when I was little, I already felt that a text was a theater, a garden in which heaps of uncontrollable, organic phenomena lay about, grew, that drawing was writing and that writing constructed things.

The proofs and their correction: there you touch upon a sore point: I have never *dared* to continue working at this stage. I feel it's utterly forbidden by editorial reprobation; I know how much it costs. Even when I correct *minimally*, I apologize profusely in the margins. I don't feel at home any more once the proofs arrive, I am a guest (same with the plays, as soon as rehearsals begin, I have no more rights).

For *Portrait de Jacques Derrida* . . . if Michel Delorme hadn't expressly requested it I would never have proposed such a layout (it existed, having been prepared for the colloquium "Judéités" on Jacques Derrida and hence Michel Delorme had it under his eyes; I wouldn't on my own initiative have put it in the book). It's like for my notes, in my notebooks. It's *that*, this *that*, these nuggets and bits of dust, that I would like to publish, but I've never desired this "for good." My-mother-within-me is probably too frugal. I'm not, however, sure that this is a good thing.

As for rewriting, which for me ties in closely with the preceding question, that of the "visuals," I mean the physical appearance of the text (my manuscripts, as you know, are multi-colored and all but illegible – whence my fascination for yours), this can be seen in the plays: witness, for example, the very instructive "Cycle des bateliers" in Tambours sur la digue: *with one hand you prune, with the other you modify the story's trajectory. My texts are constructed by alluviation, bits of paper pasted on. Consequently we are diametrically opposed, mirror images in some way. What about your other prose texts (aside from the plays)? Do you tend when you reread them to add to them or to trim them back?*

From the beginning I was seduced, charmed, by the look of your work-in-progress; your pages are lovely, like quick paintings, I feel the great painter within you moving around beneath the paper. I like this enormously, it's become for me a necessary and indissociable aspect of your text. I myself, however, only paint with words. Wherever I write it grows dark. I drill tunnels.

I don't write in many colors as you do. Any variations are contained in the graphics: I write small, big, hurried, sometimes saturating the pages sometimes flinging down a fistful of notes, this in the prehistoric period. When the text is well established (it's always a matter of a page or two, I write in spurts) it calms down. At that point, *according to* the books, additions turn up. Certain manuscripts, among the oldest, in particular, are full of additions on pasted-on bits of paper. Next, out of "altruism," I would try to copy out or cut-and-paste, to spare the person who did my typing (who was, for a long time Marguerite, now, for the past ten years, Fatima[28]). Rewriting is not something I'm familiar with: as I told you, I "rewrite" before, I pre-write in my head, before I reach the page. However, in the matter of details, I cross out and substitute, when it comes to certain words that I feel disobeyed my call.

In the case of plays, I work completely differently. First I write a minimum of three or four versions of a scene, one after the other over two or three days: that is, I write, I let the draft rest, I return to it a day later, I go further and deeper.

---

[28] [HC's footnote in the original French text.] Marguerite Sandré and Fatima Zénati have kept me and my seminar company from our beginnings together and they turn up regularly in my dreams.

This is the first stage. At another stage, very distant, the scene undergoes an unlimited and seismic number of mutations brought on by the collision or friction with the staging. This can take me a long way, up to ten, fifteen, twenty versions. In which one sees the lability of the theater, everything is subject to change, especially because there are characters and (1) the characters themselves are subject to dozens of alterations (sex, age, function); (2) the scene being deployed among different Variants can also go in dozens of different directions, as in life. By analogy: read the notebooks of the genesis of *The Idiot* or *The Possessed*, and you see the same process: an ongoing, unbounded flow of possibilities sifting through Dostoevsky's mind.

THE FEAR OF NAMES

We come now to the 1980s. With Ananké *and* Vivre l'orange *it seems to me that there's something new afoot, something I don't yet know how to define (perhaps I will learn by questioning you). A writing in blood like certain oranges. And a lightness which shows up in* Limonade tout était si infini, *to which we shall return later.*

I don't know, maybe you're right as reader-diviner to see "something new" at this place and time. For me there's a split between these two texts. *Ananké* still belongs to the experimental stage you took note of. It is also very structured, as far as I recall, by analytical references, the replaying of concepts I was enjoying de-trans-figuring. Shall we say there's a ludic and literary dimension that is, deliberately, absent from *Vivre l'orange*, a text I consider a manifesto of sorts: I might compare it – in its brevity, its exaltation, its affirmation – though I have never ever made this connection before (it comes to me as I write), to *Rire de la Méduse*: both somewhat proclamatory texts, like indications of directions and perhaps magical *"wishful thinking."*[29] With regard to blood, *Portrait du soleil*, I believe, begins with a blood orange. In my strictly private escritoire I have always associated the blood orange with Mémé, my Oran grandmother, who loved them – I did too. I was fascinated and I took the word literally, the word and the fruit, the word as veined fruit.

Picked up again 12 November 2001

The orange, through Oran, through Mémé too, was my Algeria. The bliss of having orange trees in our garden at the Clos-Salembier (at least three or four or five!). The word "orange," such a wealth of meanings, and even more in all languages, *or* [gold], *ange* [angel], ang(st), arrange, etc. The blood also, believing it juice, I was able to love it. Not now though, when it has become tragic, too Greek, too Afghan, too tuberculous.

You speak of lightness: if I understand you, I have to wonder. Doesn't this "lightness" come from the subject's effacement? The effacement of the "me," the "self," relegated to the background there, and allegorized? These texts are more philosophical, more meditative than the preceding ones, wouldn't you say?

By "lightness" I also meant: transparency, as in dragonfly wings, but we'll come back to this. Still about Limonade tout était si infini, *I had some questions to start with about the title, not just for this book, but about your long titles in general: this title contains two titles, with no split or separation between the two elements. This happens again in* Or, Les letters de mon père, *for example, or*

---

[29] In English in the original French text.

Benjamin à Montaigne, subtitled Il ne faut pas le dire, or again in Préparatifs de noces au-delà de l'abîme, a nice alexandrine. What makes certain titles tend toward the verset, whereas you also have single-word titles, abrupt ones like Tombe *or* Déluge? *Titles with one, two, or three terms – does this depend on the number of elements that enter into the book? In* Limonade. . . *(forgive the abbreviation!) we have two elements or parts which respond to one another, "The first letter" and "The last phrase," which correspond perhaps to the two elements in the title.*

You draw my attention to the titles. The title(s) – an enormous mystery, I agonize over them. I don't have titles, as I was telling you. I am unentitled. Is this a way to feel myself without letters of nobility or nationality? Could be. I'm afraid of titles. In the title, there is also a sort of arrest, something arrested, a verdict, a designation. It's done. It's the last word. I want the title not come from "me" but from elsewhere, like the first word of the first reading.

Doubtless I'm forever trying to extract myself from the title, to undermine it, to subtitle it, make it oscillate. This one-for-the-unpindownable-whole bothers me. I'm better with titles that spill over. But from the point of view of readers this is not good: it doesn't give the reader the possibility to call a book (or a play) by its name, adopt it. So sometimes I suppose I give in to the necessity (of others) for a proper name. Or a shock, a blow: *Tombe, Déluge,* they fall, they hit. But there's no hard and fast rule. It doesn't depend on the number of elements in the book. And since the title doesn't come along until after the book, coming from it, and sometimes very late (I still don't know what *Le Récit* is going to be called), it escapes from the book like a sigh, a sigh of regret. Or a burst of laughter. The book could get along without it. Then it accepts the yoke, while trying to play with it to the limit. Shake it up. Then it submits to the judgment of God, which liberates it from its submission.

Only *Dedans*, I don't know why, didn't torment me. It was obvious, and I was still new enough in literature not to persecute it with my fears and dissatisfactions. And then, there's something tomb-like in putting a name on the slab of the book. Each time I think I see the face of my father's tomb. Whereas when it resembles a sentence, it's as if it were the first page. "Limonade" pleases me in itself, quite apart from the book. "Limonade" pleases me infinitely *in French*. But the phrase is a quotation from one of Kafka's last sighs. Similarly *Préparatifs* recalls Kafka's *Preparations for a Country Wedding*. See how close and how visible he is. God, on the other hand, is not visible.

Addition summer 2002, Arcachon

Hence mostly I wait for the divinity or the god of the text to intervene; this always happens at the last minute, the manuscript is already in the publisher's hands, and one day a voice dictates "it" to me. There you have it. I submit on the spot. This is somewhat biblical. It's like those places which owe their names to a higher jurisdiction.

Your title is often a phrase or sentence in itself, such as those I've cited, a phrase which enlarges the book without being in it. We could call it a macrophrase, an exponential word, which has more importance than all the others because of its prominent position on the cover, ahead of the book. And this nomination pulls the book along in its wake. That's how I understand your reluctance to baptize it.

DRAGONFLIES

Tel qu'au fil des glaïeuls le vol des libellules
(As over gladioli dragonflies flit)

– Rimbaud

I spoke of lightness: I also meant transparency. Things do seem to me to evolve in that direction from Limonade tout était si infini on, *even if one is still far from the "running writing" (as one says running water) characteristic of your books today. By "transparency" I mean: quest for the lightest phrasing, "dragonfly" you say at the time, and fluidity. "What I have to say is in the realm of lightness itself" (p. 17), in a sort of skimming consciousness, which seems to take place without turning back, ideas and sensations linked throughout the book without any narrative thread in the traditional sense: "I happen to myself a little strangely. A simplicity happens to me" (p. 51).*

About lightness and dragonflies: the dream of *Limonade. . .* was those sorts of absolute sentences, detached absolved in which a whole lifetime is precipitated in its final breath. The title as I was saying is the translation of one of Kafka's last sentences, scribbled on his deathbed. Each of those sentences is a masterpiece of grace. I never reread them without tears welling up. They show concern for the other and nostalgia. But: one only attains such powerful lightness at death's edge. They are apparitions and farewells, and all, and so alive. I said this "was" the dream of this book. . . But this is always my dream, a dream which can only be realized in the future, so I feel nostalgia for the future and ultimate things. It is "in the end," during the last days of the last day, that one is granted the right to grace, when you have no accounts to render to anyone any more. One is free.

In confiding this to you let me say that however violently

imperatively free I may be, I don't have that kind of freedom. I am (still) supervised, fettered, threatened. . . By whom? You know them, all kinds of "censors." To go toward the light, the naked – is also to make oneself more vulnerable, more tenuous.

There is also, as you said, the erasure of the subject, even in the grammatical sense. Little by little the pronoun disappears: "Tried to think of phrases and sentences that are almost inarticulate . . ." (p. 16), "Closed her eyes . . . Remained with her eyes closed . . ." (p. 46, then throughout). As in Le Livre de Prométhéa *the following year (1983), the punctuation becomes less elliptical.*

As also in Prométhéa *and in the essay "La Venue à l'écriture," almost contemporaneous with it, you reflect upon the book and its* mise en abyme, *instructions for its use, description of the work and its purpose: ". . . she was writing in principle to get closer to reality [. . .]. But sometimes felt herself too distant, held back, and reality went away . . ." (p. 138). The distancing comes also, it seems to me, from the use of "she" to signify "I."*

I have a tendency to do this, when it's about a *she*, an I who is not completely me, a little distant, a little off to one side, a little observed, disaffected, past or future, and who might be – I was led to think this in Rennes during a debate about *Voiles* – either my myopia, my stranger, or as seen by myopic I, a person who I am (not) still (yet) and not completely.

This third-person business is probably more frequent than I myself know. This person takes the place of the first each time that there is non-adhesion, a gap, between me and myself. It appears also in *Le Jour où je n'étais pas là*. She is (not) me or no longer me. The complete suppression of the pronoun comes from Latin, from those languages in which the verb acts or suffers, with the subject nestled, hidden, somewhere in the action.

In Limonade. . . *your thinking about the masculine–feminine also grows more explicit (and there I admit I feel a slight uneasiness, despite the rhetorical quotation marks and my feeble view of "men," perhaps because I don't feel myself to be that sort of man): "Also learned on this occasion in what way 'women's' mistakes are good and different from those of 'men,' were not 'sins' or bad deeds . . ." (p. 95), ". . . it's in the interest of 'men-men' not to dream so as to be more comfortable in the world [. . .] it's in the interest of men to hurry up and over-exist, quick-quick, eyes dead ahead [. . .] because after them the deluge . . ." (p. 97).*

SLIGHT UNEASINESS THE MASCULINE

New York, November 20–Paris, November 21, 2001

I hope that my "slight uneasiness" doesn't shock or offend you. . .

First, from the bottom of my heart I understand it, next your uneasiness didn't in the least trouble me, since I was conscious of the pedagogical nature – in the interest of others, readers – of your question: I didn't take umbrage, *hombre!*, and to ramble on, I don't see what could come between us, since we are calmly at work like children building castles in the sand. A pity I couldn't reassure you immediately, in person – but I was off in Brittany.

Masculine–feminine, etc. (1) This was part of the times, a time of struggle and opposition. (2) This is, as I am always careful to say, *in quotation marks*: in other words, my remarks turn up as quotations, as names, and not as beings, and they designate beings or persons seen from the viewpoint of sexual difference (as an aspect of sexual differences), bearing in mind the huge and heavy bibliography which thus dichotomizes us (see the

Bible and its offspring). This is also why I came to distinguish men without quotation marks, hence spilling over the bounds of words and definitions, men-men comfortably protected, blinkered, proclaimed, affirming themselves as such instead *of* letting themselves go, allowing themselves to be woman, child, cow, horse, or cowhorse. (In Brittany I always want to be born again as a cow for a little while, yet another dream.)

As soon as one becomes aware of the inevitability of these oppositions and of the usual binary ways of thinking and speaking in everyday life, one no longer can see how to keep all these things apart, these beginningless endless particles of feminine and masculine in each and every being; and it's from this difficulty in respecting the fluidity, the interchangeability, the dance, the trance, the difficulty assumed and textually relayed that certain glorious literary inventions arise: Proust's whole lexicon of *being* and *person* (which designates a "whole" person or a fragment of person, the eyes, the hands, or individuals of a species other than human, etc.). Or again, in Genet, the endless gender play that make the attributes of masculinity all feminine: for example, in *The Thief's Journal*, a virtual wedding scene between two legionnaires whose virile parts (*virilité* is feminine in French) are two spouses. Subterfuges, substitutions, metamorphoses, slippages of gender, all the resources of written and oral French come into play.

Above all, the question of "where" comes to the fore: "Didn't yet know entirely what. But already knew she knew where" (Limonade. . ., p. 176); "Among all these questions, the question of where is the most important" (p. 51). We'll come back, I think, to the "where" that seems to me to designate "Algeriance" – your Algerian origin. In short, the upshot of these new apparitions is, as I said, that I sensed a sort of turning point at this time (or "period" in the pictorial sense) in your writing, a turning point that starts with the Orange of Oran, which is to become the Oranje: I glimpse you heading toward "something else." Did you feel at that time, the early 1980s, a need to go elsewhere?

Where: this is matter of some importance to me. I think it all begins with the where. In the theater, this is irrefutable: the place, the scene, determine the whole play and its voyage. As if place had magic power. Knowing where one wants to be born, to have been born, and where to die.

Where else to go? I definitely do believe that in the 1980s I must have wanted to go somewhere else, right away. In the 1980s, or already a little before this, my eternal elsewhere had probably retracted, withdrawn into a too-inaccessible distance, too distant for any contact with the real, I was dreaming of an elsewhere that wouldn't be merely desired, messianic, textual. A little like the unhoped-for Clarice Lispector. It began with: "get away," get away from myself. Moreover I did really get away somewhere else for a few years, with Ariane Mnouchkine, into Asias, into theater, into games of the imagination and into reality. Your sense of this is spot on, I vitally needed to believe that there was an elsewhere. Or that elsewhere somewhere existed. All the elsewhere: ethical, psychic, sexual, spiritual, political. . . This was an old need, but it had grown impatient, pressing, anxious. And when one can't match one's need of elsewhere to some figure in reality, one is left with a posthumous elsewhere.

I am not at present beset by such imminences.

PRETERITIONS

December 2001–December 2004

To return to Limonade tout était si infini *and* Le Livre de Prométhéa: *numerous scenes that show up again in the first person and in greater detail in your recent books are here recounted in the third person. A few examples, taken at random:*

"Her mother had told her: 'you shall not touch your body. You can go mad'" (Limonade. . ., *p. 104);*

"She'd had the experience of the botched child" (p. 64);

"She sat laughing on the staircase's top step . . ." (p. 32) (staircases often link the floors of your books!). And yet again, in Benjamin à Montaigne. . .: *"July was the month when the light is so limpid that one could almost see to eternity through it . . ." (p. 24). July, the writing month. Always, the texts are marked by it, branded.*

". . . because it's at night that one is able to discover the other world at the same time" (p. 30). So the night is made light, the oneiric world indicated in all your books as a wellspring for writing, for creation (in 2003 your dream book, Rêve je te dis, *spotlights this; it brings a new kind of light, new sticks and stones to the edifice).*

*Or again, sentences that at times call to each other almost word for word or telescope each other, meteors, years apart. As in: "Nothing would make us so anxious as continuous happiness, unless it was the discovery that our beloved bliss would suffer in the long run were it not threatened. We are made for fragments of eternity cut to our size. [. . .] I am floating because it is so beautiful this morning . . ." (*Prométhéa, *pp. 105-6), which, sixteen years later, becomes: "It's because it is too beautiful, we can't bear it. Beauty makes me want to die in your arms" (*Or, Les lettres de mon père, *1997).*

Rereading you later, therefore, one feels that one has already read these things: why is it one has the impression that you only began to say them years later, that there was a gradual unveiling (this is one of the connotations, as we said, of the title Voiles*)? Is it that the corpus has become more openly self-referential (I know you dislike the term "autobiographical") – as one may deduce from the phrase "the essential of what I was trying to say is true"*

100

(Prométhéa, p. 105)? Does it arise from the weight of the implicit, from the unsaid, the unsayable, the that-which-"one must not say" at last revealed? Might some people's difficulty in reading you come from that, from the unsaid, from what mustn't be or what you couldn't/didn't want to say? How do you analyze the reticence that followed your early and immediate recognition (with the Médicis Prize for Dedans*) and finally vanished, as people got used to reading you, giving you, finally, renewed recognition today?*

The recurrences escape me. It's you who bring them out. As an experienced "reader" – and not as a forever blind and ignorant author – I would say all this comes from a depth(s) my writing draws on almost always without my knowledge. This depth(s) is constituted of a multitude of primitive "things": scenes, affects, traces, recurring experiences in my work and in literature in general. Certain "things" I could give twenty or thirty different translations or versions, that is, readings, of. In the same way I return to certain pages of Dostoevsky or Proust or Stendhal and realize that they've been so pored over and embroidered upon that I am extracting an nth reading, still totally original. Time, history, political events – which are never "strictly" political for they come to us also as personal metaphors – states of mind whose intensity fluctuates, color, dolor, all this works to make the alreadysaid once again the neverbeforesaid. For example: I only began to "understand" the pane, the last sheet of glass between me and my father dying, decades later, it was still there, then it began to turn up, slip in elsewhere, into other circumstances, etc.

The unveiling of which you speak is therefore in my view caused by a "natural" process, a maturation which can only take place over time and with repetition, as if one saw a volcanic eruption or an assassination first as blurred, then little by little one's sight adjusts, focuses, and in the end one distinguishes the drops of fire or blood. One becomes more

101

"intelligent," less bewildered, more apt to recognize. It's that flock of turkeys I saw in a field at Kerala, never had I seen any so big and so free, and flying, until, getting closer, I realized it was a flock of vultures digesting like cows.

Experience also helps the craft of writing; little by little I learn, I integrate manners, actions, maneuvers, turns of phrase, accelerations, a whole apprenticeship of stylistic devices which become more immediate for me, more familiar.

"The difficulty in reading you" (I believe Jacques Derrida addressed this question definitively in *H.C. pour la vie*): I myself no longer see more of the unsaid or of the said, for I know all too well that "saying" also hides. "Reticence" – that long period – it will be better analyzed in the future, or forgotten, I have no idea which. I always vaguely thought I was seen as "inexcusable," as if I was doing something bad which was good, or something-good-which-was-bad, as if therefore I was accused or suspected of reveling in some delectable, inaccessible thing – therefore masturbatory to my mother's way of thinking. But that's the least of it. There is: the ultra-poetic use of the language – and what's more by a woman; intelligence – and what's more in a woman; independence, non-integration into a school, phalange, movement, party, house (of publication, etc.), the charges against me are countless. My accusers, however, are rumor mongers: they *have never read me*.

People are often surprised too to discover that I am "nice" (they have a counter-image of hardness which goes along with intellectual strength), a modern version of the taboo woman, witch, etc. The old story. Or the accusation of phallic femininity.

My voice is a surprise too.

In short there has been an army of phantasm-clichés, which time slowly dissipates.

Your most recent books feel as if they'd been constructed linearly, in one fell swoop without redrafting or retouches; perhaps this comes from your Stendhalian side, this sort of ongoing dictation, made explicit in the 2001 Le Récit/Manhattan: "*I write what comes, without explanation*": "*I wrote this question as it came, I noted the expression 'evidence' and I didn't touch it.*"

As for the cryptic, whose obscurity can be at times Mallarméan or like Paul Celan, I believe that to read you in 1970 or in 1980 it sufficed (sufficient but necessary!), as I have said from the start, to learn your Cixaldian language – one learns to read you by reading you, you who write "in tongues," tongues foreign to the tongue. As I indicated in my preceding question, your writing seems to evolve (I date this, albeit uncertainly, from Le Livre de Prométhéa, *whose arrival was heralded a year earlier, in 1982, by* Limonade tout était si infini*) toward transparency, not abruptly, but in a gradual stripping away without any concession to common, everyday language.*

The "linear" construction of which you speak is only apparent. *Le Récit* turned up as a frightful mishmash. I had no idea what to make of it. I've forgotten, I see, to tell you its name – at last "received" from the gods and transmitted to my publisher Michel Delorme. It is to be called:

Manhattan
Lettres de la préhistoire.

This business of the title that I must wait for, that doesn't come along, that doesn't come along, until it comes, is a perfectly plausible metaphor for the work that goes on inside me when I write: the pages, sentences, phrases, themes pile up, mute but weighty in my head, for months and days until it all bursts into words.

The evolution you detect from *Limonade* on – might it also have to do with the discipline (hair shirt and discipline) the theater required of me, which ran contrary to my original direction? It's not impossible.

There are also the seminars, a discourse I believe powerful, but uttered, projected.

Next:

(1) I already no longer remember *Le Récit/Manhattan* in detail, but is it really linear? It seemed to me on the contrary to be threatened on all sides, backing off, twisting and turning, etc.

(2) The "Mallarméan" (which was never close to me) of which you speak, let's say the elusive, the evasive, I only see this clearly in two or three texts full of flights and fear, like *Portrait du soleil* or *Les Commencements*. But other texts (*La, Illa*) are merely, or so I imagine, set in places books no longer go (the unconscious, dreams, the imaginary) but where, once when they went along after the dead, they went without a second thought (as in the Bardo Thodol, the Tibetan Book of the Dead). And what about certain moments in Montaigne, all beautifully complicated [*tarabiscotés*]. Tarabiscot: a groove separating a strip of molding from a smooth part – what a word!

And, it seems to me, all this comes back to the matter of scale [*échelle* or, in English, "ladder"] (what a word! what words!) and echelons, or rungs: as if I went up and down the ladder that traverses the sphere of writing, perching sometimes near the crust sometimes closer to the kernel. It seems to me – I am not sure of anything (save that I'm sure I'm not sure of anything).

The ladder [*échelle*: feminine] the staircase [*escalier*: masculine]: impossible to get away from them – my feminine/masculine spinal cords. First, they turn up all the time in my dreams, I climb I don't get anywhere, I fly, I crawl. Next or first they've always been there, in my realities. No (house, abode, shelter) without the spiral, the risers, I see myself (I see my body) (my mind) in Oran (in Algiers = trees, ladders), in Arcachon, traversed, articulated, borne, oriented haunted, by stairs. My brother and I seated on the bottom one.

And always, at the top, pirouetting and somersaulting, the squirrel.

Thoughts' props – absolutely vital for my writing soul. You have seen true. I have a physical – physicamental – sensation of stories, levels, discrepancies, gaps, splits, mostly located on the up/down vertical plane etc. I must have been monkeysquirrel in another life. I always see myself looking out from a high point (insofar as my myopia allows this) less space than time, unreeling.

But the Earth goes round, not too badly

New York, January 24–Paris, January 25, 2002

I have been in mourning. Hence my silence. Since our last conversations the wheel has turned and here we are in the second year of this new century which has got off to a very bad start, despite all our hopes for it, above all that it be different from the century "seamed with camps," as you described the twentieth century. What do you have to say about the present state of the world?

But the Earth goes round – not too badly – I tell myself at the pleasure I feel at seeing once again the planet with which you stamp your lovely pages (their crossings out as beautiful as writing) and rediscovering your "hand" – I see, in the bands of shade cast by the shutters, the text that I cannot see without a pang, the eternal beds for dogs, and this page, therefore, which comes as a new sign of life, or a sign of re-life, is also in mourning in memory of dogs (all animals are my animals) and grandmother – mine too, both of mine are evoked, those first scenes in which one starts to lose the body of the mother.

I have a touch of the flu, as I can tell by the vagaries of

my handwriting, please forgive me – so yesterday evening, discovering your lines and your voice, my pleasure was heartfelt, and this despite and despite, despite the adieux, the changes the desolations. For – and already in response to your question – I am guided by "despites" in my vision of the world: despite the ill will of just about everyone, I am still able to feel the benefits that luck and the miracles embodied in certain people reserve, even for the heartsick like me. I am always counting my blessings, marveling that there are any, and admiring the resources of the human universe, my forever-unlooked-for "inheritance," immeasurable, without any figure of hope, and who one day turns up, as you did.

The state of the world – I don't believe it will ever improve. I long ago found myself at the point of acquiescing in its tragic structure. When I was small, I must have thought (before I was ten years old) that the Good would triumph. I think that history (History) is afflicted with the demon of repetition, a repetition with differences. Evil (and evildoers – who hold power and are the majority) is inevitable and ineradicable at its root. One suppresses one outbreak of plague. Evil invents a new plague. Yes, the twentieth century was seamed with camps (I saw them as a huge skin with barbed wire stitching), and the twenty-first century will be lacerated, wounded, stabbed with other technologies. One only changes the instruments of blackmail, servitude, and torture. And scapegoats, each time a people is massacred in place of another. That's how things work.

Can one halt the repetition, throw a wrench in the machine? For me this is the question that stands for "hope." The hope, I don't have, that is at the most an incessant search for lines of flight. What I am sure of, I regret to say, is that "the world" will always be "world" [*monde*], *mundus*, "proper, clean," appropriating, eliminating, devouring, purifying, excluding – that there will always be "the two worlds," as the naïvely prophetic sign over my grandfather's tobacco shop on the Place d'Armes in Oran proclaimed – one, hence, the dominant, the one which is now the globalizer; the other, the *impure* [*immonde*], the hounded out, the marginalized, the "filthy" of the clean, and which is composed of people or classes considered, on the political level, as the "damned" of the period; but – and this matters a great deal to me – also on the cultural level composed of the "rich" in spirit, the intolerable, the poets, philosophers, seekers of the absolute, all those whose sources of delight are found at pretty inaccessible altitudes, who live on languages, and who have found Kleist's second innocence, who desired not power but the poem, and who are hated or feared because they are not aligned and don't conform to the spirit of imitation and predation.

However, there are few such – hence few poems. But this few is immense, infinite, and I ask nothing more. No need to hope. On the other hand one must resist fatigue and discouragement. (Our writing this "book," buoyed by the swell, stopping and starting, under a fresh breeze, is a modest form of resistance. It demands an adhesion, *that surpasses us*, to literary love.)

OUR CENTURIES

How do you see your relationship with the nineteenth century viewed from the point of view of its outstanding literary movements: Futurism, Surrealism, the Nouveau Roman? I mean: where do you locate your work after/alongside/in the prolongation of this series of "movements"? In outer field? In negative? As an echo? Here I am reformulating a question that I've asked already, and that I ask again from a different perspective. . .

An intimidating question: it makes me see the extent to which I don't locate "myself" at all. I would say that I am (in my eyes) not "in outer field" but off-line, without lineage, without relationship, without ties. Not in negative either; so far as these movements are concerned I am the passerby who sees them from afar, without being affected, without being called or moved. I am and I come from elsewhere. It's not a question of rupture. Surely it's a matter of origin, or origins. I *almost* tell myself (I am trying to look back over my shoulder at the century) that the "movements" you mention are "French" – whereas I belong to a species that has (not) (yet) (ever) arrived, I'm one of those eccentric, beyond-the-pale mixtures that set up camp at gates to the City.

I asked you this, indeed intimidating, question about the great movements of the past century because these past few weeks, rereading Préparatifs de noces au-delà de l'abîme *(1978) and* With ou l'Art de l'innocence *(1981), I told myself that there was a sort of taking the opposite tack or thumbing your nose at the Nouveau Roman (which ended up becoming an embalmed literary movement, say by the 1971 Cerisy Conference – some, Michel Butor, for instance, didn't get it wrong and had by then long given up writing novels, no matter how "new"), but that there was also a natural affinity in you with Surrealism and Lautréamont. A style of writing not automatic, certainly, but perfectly free and* natural. *But maybe I'm wrong, and perhaps this is simply hindsight.*

(1) I *believe* you. I believe, since you say you detect it.

(2) I *confess*, to you, I must confess: no sooner had I read the Nouveau Roman than I let it drop. Without enthusiasm, without regret. I neither invested in it, nor detested it. I read a book by each writer, maybe two, more of Nathalie Sarraute, whom I also knew "in reality." And I didn't linger. It's just that I have hardly anything to see or find on their respective

paths, my heart has never throbbed, no sentence ever pierced my heart or head. So there you go. No antipathy. If perchance I'm given a fragment to read, I appreciate – off in the distance where all that remains for me. No kinship. Whereas I do feel that, had I lingered, I'd have had an affinity with certain surrealist writings – perhaps – for your questions lead me to notice, from another point of view, my attitudes of old, unanalyzed at the time – since they were me. So I see myself, looking back now, the way I lived, *where* I lived in literature in those days. What was I reading? Who was I speaking to? To Kafka, to Kleist, Shakespeare, Milton, to Freud or Derrida, but finally, aside from Rimbaud, I didn't spend much time dreaming in France and this didn't bother me. I have always been in a foreign country in my own home. I remember having read Aragon with pleasure, or Éluard a little, things I read before I was twenty, then I went away, for me all that smelled of Paris, good society, not that I was dogmatic about it.

Some writing survived my flights: Gracq, for example – whom I always read as a sort of German romantic metamorphosed into a professor. Gracq escaped from himself.

Again, going back a century, I imagine that you feel as close to Lautréamont as to Rimbaud or Stendhal. Does this mean that one may situate you at the opposite pole from the maniacal writing of a Flaubert, very far from Hugo, too, for example?

Going back in time I feel better, for it is easier to situate myself among the time-detached, *the dead outliving those who are the inhabitants of literature.*

Lautréamont: I had a moment of love, at puberty (mine). Since then, nothing more. I tell it the way it is: I never went back. Who knows why.

Flaubert: no, I don't place myself at the opposite pole. He

has visions I experience as of a fabulous violence (I adore the *Tales*, I believe them). He's not a friend. But a writer whose craft I respect and whose linguistic adventure I find necessary and inseparable from our common legacy. I am extremely grateful to him for his work on the phrase, the sentence, syntax. For me, he is the inventor. Obviously in the case of Hugo I inverse: I like him, he could be a friend, I marvel at his cardiac capacities, I find him archi-contemporary and he exasperates me with his clichés, his redundancies his French smithy-ing. But, French literature being by and large ultra-reactionary bourgeois misogynist racist (Flaubert, Baudelaire, and almost all of them right to the present day), I bless him for his activism. Otherwise one would forget the ethical and political damage done by literature, which time in passing pardons, but not me. Luckily there was Hugo, active against capital punishment, his different kinds of courage. As for the rest, I read his choleric prose texts more than his poems or novels. But this is immense.

I expressed myself badly: I wanted to speak of Hugo in his phraseology and his "emphasis," his grandiloquence or "emphrase" to forge a cixaldism. And I mentioned Flaubert, of the utmost importance as well despite his work's constriction, for his obsessive documentation.

Flaubert, his obsessive documentation: I'm not obsessive to that degree, but I love the vast caverns, all the grottoes, towers, galleries, libraries, workshops, all of that. My caverns are more bookish: from the start I have amassed my literary emotions, and to borrow from Rousseau his "verbiage" or his "herbiage," my "documents" and traces are the scenes, phrases, verses I have wept over (I still weep – as I am still in the grip of the same musical phrases, Mahler, Gluck, Beethoven, etc.).

"Obsessive documentation" interests me just as the inscriptions on Montaigne's tower do.

THE SHELVES

To come back to you after this detour through the nineteenth century, already so distant (in many ways the sixteenth century is closer to us), what is your relationship to documentation, encyclopedias, libraries? During the writing of your last book, which focuses on a memory of New York in the 1960s, you asked me to send you some maps of Manhattan – for your fiction writing do you do other kinds of research (archives, etc.)?

A fascinating question. I can't give a single answer: I have no principles and each book is a case in itself. One thing I can say for sure: no libraries (except my own). And also this, a matter of "climate," of environment. As you know, I write in my forest hideout, far from the world, and in a dream. I avoid outside intrusions. I asked *you* for the New York maps because you are in the secret of the writing. When I write I confide *in no one*. I can't say a word, *don't wish* to say a word about what I'm doing, what moves me, gives me life and delight. Because it would break the spell. When I am spellbound I fear for the spell's frail skin. So I move and express as little as possible.

What is always *there*, always already there, is my personal library, on my mind's shelves, the beloved too numerous to count (from Homer to Jacques Derrida), whom I know by heart and consult. This isn't "research," it's conversation. I ask Montaigne what he thinks "about it," and he responds. Or Dostoevsky. This is my oldest habit. I have always *lived* this way. Sometimes I feel the need of a piece of *information*. Or maybe (*Le Jour où je n'étais pas là*) I obtain (with difficulty) medical books from my brother.

For a specialized term (for example, the strange attractors) I get my son Pierre-François to give me a lesson in mathematics.

For the rhetorical analysis of a sentence I might question my daughter, a remarkable poeticist.

The role of dictionaries: I always think of the dictionary (my fuel). I have a huge collection of dictionaries, in as many languages as necessary (Latin, Greek, Russian, Portuguese, etc.) and in as many fields as I could desire (rhetoric, poetics, stylistics, mythology, psychoanalysis, etymology), which I consult abundantly. And the foundation, always there, the good old encyclopedias, Larousse of the nineteenth century, etc.

Documentation: books, journals, magazines on Osnabrück or Oran, or Algiers or. All this gets transfigured, displaced.

Often the text telephones me: requests information. This summer, for example, on the track of Elpenor, I reread Homer, the various versions of the *Odyssey* and the Greek (with the help of my Greek professor friend, Claudine Bensaïd). Sometimes it's paintings I scrutinize (Rembrandt, for instance) having *seen* them in reality in museums, but at the moment of writing, using reproductions.

There must be other things as well – I like it a lot when the concrete comes to my aid, the immemorial memory of the here-and-now or the archives. Those *maps*[30] you sent me, I examined them with a magnifying glass, every which way, and in a certain manner, I inhabited them for a while. It's theatrical staging, a kind of map I set under my writing feet.

Your response excites me, it grips me because I work in an entirely opposite way on one point: the "secret" of the writing. I myself hand

---

[30] In English in the original French text.

out bits of text to read left and right, I publish fragments and even entire extracts. The book remains on the block, on the loom for a long time.

As I was saying, I don't give mine out to read, and I don't expect and don't wish any commentary. My ideal readers can be counted on the fingers of one hand, and I leave them the liberty to approach my text when they will but without them ever getting ahead of me. In the end I can almost say that my vital, my unique reader is the one who gives the book its title, the book itself in other words. I am pretty much at peace in these regions, as if everything were taking place in a dream.

How do you feel today about L'Art de l'Innocence, *otherwise called* With, *which came out at the beginning of the 1980s? Why are the titles abbreviated on the cover – which is what you did before subtitles came along?*

Today, *I don't know* (a frank answer: humble). *With* remains for me a climate, a long plunge into reverie – it doesn't, I believe, have any model, though *today* and not then I could compare it with the technique of the "solitary promenade." That was a period with neither hero nor heroine, other than the "infinitesimals," little things, feathers, light but essential debris. Title/or/subtitle: much might be made of your hints. But first of all: this was not theorized, nor explicitly decided, I no longer know even how this came about. On the other hand it brings out the tension of the uncertainty among the terms which dispute the title, the throne, the identity, etc., my eternal impossibility, my natural penchant for the undecided, and still today this goes on, a title for me floats or rather manifests itself at the head of a fleet of titles, and it is the reader-secret-book which pilots the ship in my place.

113

Add that I needed to use a word (*with*) that was utterly impossible in French, unpronounceable inaudible, etc.

New York–Montsouris, January 28–30, 2002

In L'Art de l'innocence *there is patience and impatience: waiting, revelation – illumination (or "inspiration," as one used to say). Is this a frequent occurrence in the (secret) moment of writing?*

Have I the right to respond only by "yes"? Sometimes you pre-read me so well that I just nod my head: yesyes.

With in effect: you write *with.* Inside and With. With T.B., C.L., and others.[31] *Is this for you a form of resistance (a way to feel less alone in the quest), these "substantial allies"?*

These "substantial allies," who accompany me guide me, you are probably correct to perceive them as auxiliaries or supplements of resistance (you are one of them, one of the allies, without whom I would be without myself). Let's say that they are also my substitute parents, my most faithful friends, my co-livers and contemporaries of the heart; I feel, what's more, vaguely guilty thinking that I have so much love for those who are absent or "dead" in appearance, that they keep me warm and enchanted so much more than many of the "present in appearance."

(Oops, here's my darling cat who, having been wakened with a start by a dream, has sat down on the paper and is rubbing against my pen, so as to defend *all* the animals.)

Still about the allies: characters from Shakespeare, from mythology, and so on. How do they turn up in your writing retreat – your

---

[31] Thomas Bernhard, Clarisse Lispector.

tower-library à la Montaigne, in the present moment of the writ-
ing: "A mid-July noon hour instead of the April one [. . .] I felt so
utterly perfect a second ago, on the balcony, in Antouylia sphere"
(With, p. 247). Do you travel with your library? Or is your library
memory-fed, known by heart?

Library-allies: I have three at least: one in the by-heart of
my head; one along my window and all around me in Paris –
the same in Arcachon. I am never without my book people.
An entire assembly, a choir, my tribe, my very young ancestors, my class my consolation, my "voices" (I'm going away
for a bit: my cat has taken all the room – I have my nose in
her right ear).

January 31, 2002

Back again: so, yes, "I travel" (= I write) always with my
library. This is one of the reasons it wouldn't cross my mind
to write "en voyage," traveling in reality. En voyage I am
en voyage, I am away from myself, I am elsewhere. When I
write I am *in* my library, or it is in me. I always come back to
Montaigne's tower; it seems to me that it depicts me, where
my mind lives, it models me. I represent myself in its shape;
so I am a sort of library, with a starry sky, a manuscript ceil-
ing. For me these surroundings are vital. I need books at
my fingertips, against my knees, in my back (like angels, not
traitors). Or on the paper like my cat.

New York, October 23, 2002

So far we've hardly mentioned the references to the Bible that
abound in your books, the most numerous references along with
the Rimbaud and Dante citations. Take, for example, Ananké,
published in 1979, in which we find: ". . . a sachet of myrrh that

115

rests between my love's breasts . . ." (p. 216); ". . . the rustling of her myrrh-anointed thighs in the vineyards flowering . . ." (p. 214); we also find the stairs linked to these resurgences from the Song of Songs: ". . . the stairs leapt, who runs down faster than my sister's hair, the black one, she who ran through the hills ahead of me, quicker than a Lebanese goat . . ." (p. 15); ". . . reach the door, the exit, the other life . . .". (Indeed, we also find, let me say in passing, friend K. and nuncle Freud, both part of your personal mythology.)

Paris, November 27, 2002

I write the date too in order to make room in this book with its company of cats, female ones, for Aletheia and Philia, who came along a month ago, sent by Thessie, and who with their twin frenzies transform my beings into jungles forests and orchestras of paws. Here I am answering the questions of October 23, which have accompanied me from Manhattan to Paris.

About the Bible: for some time already my readers, or some readers, have at last been heeding the presence of this book whose trace you, of course, have not failed to pick up. Bible has been with me from the most distance times. Was it my first book? The old very old scruffy Haggadah come from Germany with Omi my grandmother, told me the *passages*, all the passages, Bible, the book of passages, crossings of seas and deserts, metapholyric of any voyage through lives and deaths, the most ancient of my themes. The characters of the Bible are the ancestors of my familiar heroes, those of Homer and of the epics, I have always known Moses, Abraham, David, Saul, the broken kings, betrayals and awestruck prophets. And I am, in fact, a (descendant) Jonas:[32] Omi's maiden name was Rosalie Jonas. The Jonases led the Osnabrück consistory.

---

[32] See note 5 above. "Jonas" is the French spelling of "Jonah".

116

Add to that I learned that my father Georges' Jewish name was Jonas too. So I was born *in* a whale and in some way I have never left it. I love the Bible. You were right to associate Rimbaud and Dante, who came along later, but who have in effect taken their place in the choir of the Cantors of my canticles.

Along with Jonah, Samson, for whom I've fallen – in love, in horror – for reasons to do with blindness humility (his) fate, the most Greek of the Hebrew heroes. Besides I've always had a complicated phantasmic relationship to hair. I myself have a mane of hair, which I cut for the first time, my father dying, thinking to please him, since then each time I try to let my old curls grow back, the scissors turn up.

The Bible is everywhere and from the beginning and "naturally" present in what I write, myths, themes, leitmotivs, songs, promised lands, philosohemes. I am "at home" in it as in the desert and with God, that is, with the need of and the lack of God.

*

In many respects La Bataille d'Arcachon *occupies a unique place among your books: it is a "tale"; its language doesn't much resemble the usual Cixaldian, if I may say so (its syntax is more classical); and furthermore the book was published in Quebec, in 1986, that is, during the period that I have mistakenly called (also in the next section, written before this one!) a time of narrative "silence." One meets some familiar characters in this book: H., Prométhéa, . . . What were the circumstances behind the appearance of such a strange book?*

La Bataille d'Arcachon is a plaything. After *Prométhéa* (1983) I wanted to stay in that absurd, ridiculous but beneficial little city created in the nineteenth century at the same time as New York! Which everyone passed through, including Joyce, but never lingered longer than two days. At the same time, Arcachon being my own lair, where I enjoy absence and anonymity, I've always hesitated to expose it.

But I had this whim: take as setting a microtown of the French southwest. Whereupon this text fell between two publishers, if I may say so, between the opening and then the re-closing of éditions Des femmes, and at a time when I myself was turning toward the theater. In Quebec, I have a very dear friend, Anne-Marie Alonzo, who leads a heroic life as writer and editor all at once. Perhaps Arcachon-in-Quebec, this detour and this voyage, responded to more than one necessity *and* to a *possibility*: that of giving a text to my Montreal friend. Today I am delighted to have done so.

Does this Bataille d'Arcachon, *in taking up once more the characters of the previous book,* Le Livre de Prométhéa, *become in some way its sequel? It belongs unquestionably, in any case, to an utterly different vein from* Manne aux Mandelstams aux Mandelas, *the next book. Who is this H. whom one could take for your doppelgänger – doppelgängerin? – were it not specified that "H. is very religious" and that she "drinks cappuccino as if it were a potion or sacred wine," which is not, to my knowledge, your case, although you do like black coffee! One could almost apply what you write in* Ananké *to this H. : "And now, I wondered, which I can say I? [. . .] I was so not me, the me I knew in the days when I lived to write. If a question were to ask me: who are you not? it would be easy to answer, there would be an I to speak of all the I's who no longer interest me [. . .]. I've so few images on the subject of me." Furthermore, one recognizes in this* Bataille d'Arcachon *certain of your concerns: "On the one hand poems only rarely allow themselves to be drawn. On the other hand in Paris H. has trouble hearing what they say. To manage to gather and polish a page of writing 21 bis avenue Gambetta, is as precarious as hearing God's heart beating . . ." (Needless to say one finds Him [God] again, p. 17.)*

This "H." is somebody inside me, who sometimes manages to manifest a childhood and a taste for everyday life, the poetry-of-going-to-the-café, which is, to the other me, practically always forbidden: no time, I live austerely, I don't even have time to *dream* of going to a café (a miniature promised land). For a few short months, this H. was liberated, and the *Bataille*'s lightness bears witness to that. I hadn't made the connection with *Ananké*, but as usual you've spotted what I didn't: both books have sprung up in the cracks, where one of my personas, usually blocked by the excessively tight weave of my obligations, has popped up. I call these emanations H., because they are a little mute, unfinished, partial. You refer to "she is very religious." Now there, I recognize her, in your reading. She's definitely the one who has the religion of daily life, so distant, so desirable, that land where my mother Ève reigns supreme.

WALLS

New York, March 22, 2002

Another fairly long interruption (almost two months – but in the meantime we have backtracked) in the interview: several trips, "displacements" in different senses of the word, flux and migrations, etc. And the world is decidedly not an easy place to inhabit these days: today it's my inner Palestine, my Jerusalem wall, my Muslim Jewishness that hurts. This pause also corresponds, in the reading that I am attempting of your work, to what seems to me a fairly radical break in your work, which I am trying to decipher: the five years of relative silence separating, in your "fictional" work, Le Livre de Prométhéa *(published by Gallimard in 1983) from the immense* Manne aux Mandelstams aux Mandelas *(back to Des femmes in 1988), five years during which you were working for the theater*

119

(five plays) and only published, in Quebec, La Bataille d'Arcachon (1986). *One reason for my question: your work, it strikes me, comes out of this long "silence" greatly transformed: anchored in immediate collectively lived life, outside the body, more "political" hence, and at the same time plunging deeply into your own life, memories, history (little by little the family past comes along, a past not simple but anterior, beginning with* Or, Les letters de mon père, *in 1997). Does this transformation (which I don't dare name metamorphosis, for of course the substrate of the whole preceding work remains, and one plainly perceives the continuity as well) come from your time in the theater, from a halt for reflection, from a change in your history?*

(1) Jerusalem–Palestine: I was supposed to go there tomorrow, with Jacques Derrida. For reasons of time the trip has been postponed (until June?). I have written, for the occasion, the short text that I enclose

(2) The causes of the "break" = turn = mutation = generalized transfer = zigzags—or *checkpoint*[33] (there are two or three clear turns in my life-work) are: multiple moves in my "private" (a word I don't like, it's the contrary of *deprived*, it's not lacking for anything, over-abundant, passionate) life; in my editorial history; in my arrival in the theater, with an important initiation period, accompanied by real (Asia, Cambodia, India) and imaginary voyages, a revolution in the givens of my world – political-poetic enlargement, alliances, that I try to put in the form of texts, between the Poet and Action, figured by the Mandelstam–Mandela couple, always my old unanswered question, *Wozu Dichter*, what's the good of poets, finally my attempt to cross-fertilize the Theater's vast stage with the subterranean stage of meditation upon the passions and the difficulty of writing in a period which remembers the great classical novel but must find another roof for other sorts

---

[33] In English in the original French text.

of characters. Writing for the theater lifted the restriction or inhibition regarding "characters" by letting me transpose strangers' voices. But I always sought for these voices an epic source, a body. My old need of heroes. Heroes: characters moved by ideas, desires, dissatisfactions, and capable, because of this, of traversing volcanoes. Basically, I admit, I have always wanted to love giants (even) small ones, prometheuses, samsons, the insightful blind, saints, prophets.

THE BODY WRITES

. . .the circulation of incredible saps. . .
– Rimbaud

To backtrack again: in Préparatifs. . . *(1978). . . which is one of the texts already designated as "fictions" in your bibliographies (before you used the term "novel"), I have the paradoxical feeling that the fictional (mythology, etc.) is dissipating: it strikes me that the itinerary, the fatigue that opens the book, and the "veiled murmur from right up close [. . .] outside lightless dreams" (p. 183) that closes it, are the evocation, in the present of the writing, of the state of the writing body.*

Préparatifs. . . : I only vaguely remember it. What I do recall is the theme of Preparations, my mental state at the time. But also an echo of all Kafka's *Preparations*, from the *Wedding Preparations, Hochzeitsvorbereitung* – right to all the *attempts* (which by definition are unsuccessful, even if they are guided by dreams). I also remember a *zone* where this text was written, the chiaroscuro dreamland between the unconscious and the flesh.

121

You ask me to "flesh out" my meager response on "state of the writing-body." I recognize that, paradoxically, in speaking of the body my formulation was somewhat wraithlike. With your permission, and lacking any desire to reacquaint myself with *Préparatifs. . .*, which has slipped from sight – I shall rather deliver myself of a few thoughts about the writing-body in general.

That I write bodily, with from through thanks to my body with the help of my entire body and all my bodies, is essential. Starting from the feeling/sensation that the exercise of writing is extremely physical, athletic sportive – and requires being in perfect "shape," as we say of athletes, that is, demands a perfect animal-like poise, balance, harmony of muscles nerves respiration brain. When I write, my whole inner machine is at work, the whole body motor, accelerator. Only my eyes and ears remain in the background, for I avoid the brakes constituted by contacts with the outside objective world. Then I set off. It's a race. A tense race, plucked strings, it must resemble the carnal intensities that come together in a sexual relationship, because there is a goal, another side to be attained. My entire body becomes language, and my thinking head makes use of my entire body.

In reality I don't always have the same body. It is more or less happy, according to thousands of factors, what I've dreamt, the state of my heart – constricted or dilated as I'm feeling more or less amorous. I count a lot on it. But on the other hand writing is always a beneficial drug, in the atrocious times (= black) of my existence, each time that I've managed to drag myself to a piece of paper, I've recollected my powers of acquiescence, of consent. This of course is due to the generally soothing effect of analyzing human things and giving form to chaos. Sublimation according to me is just this: managing to put a human face on whatever first appears to us as not human or inhuman.

Among the experiences in or of my body that I've had, I'll note two in particular: one is that of the incandescent body, eroticized, which furnishes a quantity of illuminations to the text, as if the overcharged sources of electricity produced flashes of lightning. So it has always seemed to me natural that certain texts be called Illuminations; the other experience is that of the body attacked, by this or that illness or alteration, a dysfunction. That happened to me, quite recently. In the text symptoms are produced in the form of themes or syntax. It's fascinating. So last year I watched an entire pulmonary world appear, complete with feelings of asphyxia, feverishness, power cuts. I was working on the lung, on TB, on lung cancer. I had acute pneumonia. For six months I couldn't shake it off. What I couldn't know (medical science, like me, not knowing) was whether by dint of working on the lungs for months, I had provoked a furious response. Whether, in my writing, "before" the pneumonia, this episode was already brewing, accompanied by early signs. Or both at once? After all if one can make oneself come, dream, forget, if one can administer writing to oneself in pleasure-forms, why not think that writing also contains hurtful powers, waiting to be conjured up.

Yet another thing: the "sleep" part of the writing activity, the biggest, the nocturnal part, does half the work for me. I go to bed *in order to* dream. Carefully. And with hope and curiosity. While I sleep, the shooting (the film, the scenarios) takes place. In the morning I harvest. At night I sometimes half-wake to sleepdream the next part of my text. This is a very fruitful intermediary state. I can also jot down nocturnal "illuminations" – phrases, key words, glitterings – with broad strokes, in the dark.

But there is also a diurnal part, small but efficacious. When I've depleted all my energy I sometimes go to bed to "think" imagine with another rhythm than the desk's high-pressure one, a floating rhythm, aswim, unhurried, when I let images, phrases come or come back, a state of alert passivity, this lasts for half an hour, I "float," and, indeed, the current bears me along and nourishes me.

A parallel question that we are gradually pursuing, that of the flux, influx, interactions, relations, since one never writes alone: what are yours with Malcolm Lowry? You don't mention him among those close to you in the interview with Daniel Ferrer, "I am first of all a reader. . .," and to my knowledge you have never spoken of him. By his "rarity," "his dry spells," he might seem poles apart from you. In the musicality of his sentences I find him close. I ask this question for autobiographical reasons: his work has had a great influence upon my life, inciting me in particular to adopt Mexican nationality. So I would like you to like him, but I feel that something keeps you apart even as it brings you close.

Imagine that I liked him a lot a lot. In my twenties. I took him for "brothersister." Why didn't I remain close to him or ever return? I'll answer twice: (1) Probably he vanished like part of that period in the ruins of my beginnings. The only explanation is a bombardment of the self that I was. (2) Retrospectively perhaps one imagined that from under the volcano he might come back or be resuscitated as you, who knows? In any case you can think in peace that I've always liked him: now I must reread him (*n.b.* 2004: I've reread him.)

A huge question, to which you've already responded, partially at least – but can one ever be sure to have answered in full, and isn't the whole life of the man or woman who writes an effort to respond to this? – where does it come from? From what alchemy, what necessity, what tangle of circumstances does your writing come? From childhood, of course . . . but do you remember the first attempt, surely long before Le Prénom de Dieu? *And afterwards what made you keep going? Michel Butor answered this question some twenty years ago, in our book* De la distance: *it comes from darkness, from something to be lit. Have you kept finished texts, which you could countersign today, texts before* Le Prénom de Dieu?

Yes this endless question, one keeps coming back to it. The act of reading: everything began with read, read, read, read = eat, run off, forget the baseness, explore the heights, take refuge, free myself from the horrors of Algeria: so it began by escaping Algeria through enchantments.

I've always wanted to write, according to my brother, who has told me he kept my first "novel," a notebook I meant for my dying father, but which I have never seen (so I was ten years old), I've always wanted to write, but naïvely, dream-ily. After that I *invented* a great deal in secondary school, conscious of doing so, with audacities, stylistic experiments. "I invented," for example, the interior monologue. I wasn't, of course, thinking at all of being a writer but writing was a source of delight and I was good.

Then between the ages of sixteen and eighteen, I *wanted* something. That came from erotic stirrings, it was impul-sive, the words were flesh, fluids, morsels. I have very strong memories of verbal appetites. But already I had a house critic, and everything went into the bin, judged, weighted, shred-ded. I've also had moments of (harmful) temptation: suddenly I've thought the only way to write was like Rousseau, but I had nothing yet to confess. Next I've thought that to be a "writer" one had to have gone up in flames at the age of seventeen (Rimbaud). When I turned eighteen it was quite a disappointment. At the time I had no taste or judgment, just volcanoes, lava, incandescences, and itches. What's more I thought I was sick, bizarre and all that I took for a masturba-tion of the soul, in that nothing could snuff out the desire to write. I was ambitionless but totally haunted. I couldn't not have. Language was the most desirable thing in the world. I say that I was reading, but in truth I was licking, I was fondling. I have never lacked desire – even as a small child – I experienced my secret affectivity in flames, without realizing that flames and languages were only waiting for me to understand their conjunctions.

Basically I've always lived in the House of Letters but it took a while for me to reside there "legally." Plus, as a child I already separated *art* from convention: so in "composing" I tried for the shattering masterpiece but in family correspondence I was writing conventionally (for literature was secret and forbidden).

MEASURES

New York, April 4–Paris, April 30, 2002

Manne aux Mandelstams aux Mandelas *(1988) is a thick book (342 pages), probably the longest you've published. However, it comes after moving away from fiction (toward the theater). And this break, as I was saying, seems significant – but can it be analyzed? Several other thick books come along later –* Jours de l'An, Osnabrück, Benjamin à Montaigne *– which strike me as being more "*filé*"[34] (I'll come back to this term in a second) – more narrative perhaps? Could a reason be formulated for this relationship between tenor/measure? Did you experience any particular difficulty in writing* Manne, *which would explain the delay, the break, the thickness? What were the circumstances, the environment?*

---

[34] *Filer*, among other things, means "to spin" (*fil* = "thread"); *filée* can mean "spun out, drawn out."

Why am I answering between two protest demonstrations? Because I have a strong feeling of unpredictability. As if we (us, here, in France) were in a race with walls in place of hurdles. You charge off, you climb and you don't know if on the other side there is earth or abyss, or wall. So in case of death I am answering.

Manne, and its thickness. Maybe because it's a double book, book of the Mandelstams and book of the Mandelas? Or because there is a story, evocations of scenes, true facts and events? I don't know.

Writing it I didn't feel difficulty, but exaltation. The eternal child that I am loves being picked up, hauled, hurtled, by "heroes" (my father's remains?) I feel love for the beings who resist, who are faithful to principle, at whatever cost. I had just studied Mandela's history and ideas, I was an activist for the anti-apartheid movements (with Jacques Derrida); but the conjunction with the resistance of Mandelstam, an immense and wonderful poet, was what allowed me to write this North–South, snow-white-fire-black book. The struggle is always the same. Ariane [Mnouchkine] and I couldn't stop talking about this, Ariane was tempted by the idea of a play on South Africa but stopped by the impossibility of finding a suitable transposition. The combination poet + politician, political fight + poetic fight is for me the ideal, the almost impossible ideal. This text's two personages were the bearers of these two virtues, in different quantities and forms. Similarly I have great tenderness for the political Victor Hugo, his unceasing engagement stirs and amazes me. Sometimes the survival of a people or their soul depends upon one human being *speaking out* and keeping his or her word.

Also in my text I put people who are our contemporaries and whose greatness is somehow strange, as if they inhabited dreams.

Perhaps one could see in *Manne* the seeds, the Manna

Man/ne/manes and the promises of books like *Osnabrück*, where there is a kind of heroisation but *without heroism*. My mother is a simple, neutral, sinless "heroine" without idea, without it being deliberate.

N.B. I'm not sure I understand what you mean by (1) *thick* [*épais*]. Thick? Can you explain? (2) "*filée*"? Is there some kind of opposition, and if so, what, connecting two words that seem to be words of consistence?

*"Épais" and "filé" are terms I employ for painting, for mine certainly: there are thick canvases, on which much matter accumulates, and others fine and liquid like washes, more attenuated in their colors, more water color, or covered only with a light glaze of oil and "Liquin" . . . So it seems to me that the syntax becomes more "*filée*"—fluid, ductile – starting with* Manne *in 1988. But perhaps this is not significant, it is a simple remark, which I haven't formalized.*

One question comes up again and again in the recent books: to die young, "not have the time" – as was the case with "yourfather" ("yourfather" says the mother), and with mine, "Ourfather" – who-art-in-Heaven, always already dead. And in Jours de l'An *(1990) all these themes are gathered up again, mixed, systematically one might say: the anniversaries, the dead child, to die young, the damned (the Mandelstams, Tsvetayeva, etc.); the mother, the father, Algeriance, etc. I set* La Fiancée juive *and* Déluge *a little apart (we'll come back to them in a moment). But the recurrence of characters has become even more systematic in recent volumes (I would happily say recent tomes, so strongly does it strike me that these are all parts of the same book):* Le Jour où je n'étais pas là, Les Rêveries de la femme sauvage, Benjamin à Montaigne. *Already, as in* Or *and* Osnabrück *(heralding a new reception, a wider recognition at last of your work, or rather the works' return to displays and windows after the thirty-year break following* Dedans *and the media attention of the Médicis Prize), the father*

and the mother change status: no longer do we have Ève as Mother
Earth and Georges wrestling the dragon (or the angel), now it's
"my father," "my mother," "my brother," "uncle so-and-so," "my
aunt." So here once more the old question: what happened? In
Beethoven à jamais *already you write: "A story without a plot,*
and with the minimum of characters" (p. 41).

So many questions, in all directions:

(1) Not have the time: one never does, right? I suffer constantly from lack of time, that is, lack of "nothing," of space, conversation with the trees, the birds, the air, the color, of living to the rhythm of "un-cultivated culture" rather than to that of "so-cultivated nature." I like the instant. Without instants, I suffocate. It's not death as halt, break, stop, that bothers me, it's not having time to breathe in life. The only thing that I manage to safeguard is nighttime, dreams, without which I would break down.

(2) The recurrence of characters: this is a freedom I have granted myself belatedly. I had the absurd feeling that one couldn't come back to them or bring them back, like some kind of stupid modesty, a "stupidesty," say. But "myfather," or Ève, are inexhaustible, like Ulysses or Hamlet or the Idiot: they are a trove of enigmas. And they are kind enough not to hide from my curiosity. They have, it seems to me, that discreetly epic dimension, the necessary fodder for human theater. Someone close to me who interests me a lot is my brother, an exceptional personnage, but obviously I don't give myself the right, nor does he authorize me, to appropriate or take possession of him. What I re/collect of him (quite a bit all the same) with his express permission is very little compared with what I see.

To the question of "what happened?" I think all I can say is this: a ban was lifted, very late, probably activated by my apprehension of the "terminal" or as Kafka would say "the ultimate": the imminence of our lives' end and what

129

this will bring with it in the way of silence, omission, efface-ment, strangulation, forgetting. So I rush, I rush, a race against death. These deaths of mine (of my mother, who is unchanged at ninety-two, the death of those who are my heart's flesh).

What separates the recent books from the preceding ones (I know, I've said this before but I repeat myself, it's an old habit, I see the caesura after Manne, *but one could also say that it took place shortly before you left Des femmes for Galilée) is, I believe, development, the passage of time (whence my reference to Proust's work), the deploying of anecdote. In the preceding books, as in (as if they were) collections of poems, there wasn't always this feeling of a thread unspooling, save that of the writing, the throes and joys of compos-ing. Would you be becoming a novelist, at long last (a novelist of your life, I mean)?*

– (The move from Des femmes to Galilée does not enter into the thematic transformations, as far as I know. This change was what Jacques Derrida would call an event: an utterly unexpected and sudden occurrence, whose conse-quences are certainly very broad, but which were unantici-pated.)

– *Time*, yes, or rather no, not "time," but all the times of time, yes, time, time and time again [*tant et tant étant*] and all the times and tempests yes, I think of them ceaselessly, and in all ways, ahead, to the side, behind, in the distance, etc. At bottom – this comes to me all of a sudden – there must be two registers within me: that of *time*; and that of *blows*, shocks, dramas, crises, amputations.

– Novelist" is a word I have always dreaded – I have no use for it, I don't know what to do with it, I am less afraid of poet, or explorer, or write-rope walker [*écrilibriste*]. "Novelist of your life" you say. But in fact, there are very few elements

130

that come from my life, that concern my *own* person, don't you find? It's characters, my family and friends, the crowds of beings who indeed create me but who are not me, who fill up the stage. My *own* life remains unknown.

TEMPO

Roosevelt Island, July 2002

We come now to the nineties of the other century. Maybe I'm mistaken; or maybe this is just a vague impression from my rereading, but I see a change of tempo in Jours de l'an *(1990), then above all in* L'Ange au secret *(1991) – which the syllable* l'an *links to the preceding book – as compared to* Manne *(*Manne / L'an / L'Ange, *there's a phonetic contiguity). Shorter scenes, a fragmentation of the discourse, as in the short stories (whereas* Manne *kept two narrative threads running parallel from end to end). Do you share this impression, and if so, what might have brought about the provisional break in the continuum that we will find again in* Or, *and also to a degree in* Déluge *and* Messie?

July 10, 2002

I am about to head off for Cerisy (Derrida),[35] grey weather, images. Cat gone wild. I begin to reply to reconnect – with the thread – with Fy[36] – with these "me's" – these texts about which you are so much more the enlightened witness than I am!

---

[35] In July 2002 there was a conference at Cerisy-la-Salle on Derrida, "The Democracy to Come."

[36] Cixous is playing on the sounds of *fil* ("thread") and *Fy*, the initials of her co-author, Frédéric-Yves Jeannet

I am struck by the things you notice that had escaped me. I find true and fascinating what you point out: *l'an, l'Ange*, etc.; the question of time, of which I know little – except: I like and I prefer – I believe – shards and fragmentations, they are how my depths mark time. I do, however, "prethink" that I have to order, tie together. In my view this is more in reaction or as a correction to the chopped-up, dislocated, allusive rhythm, in which I take pleasure. But? Is it true? Texts that are broken, fleeting, correspond surely also to urgencies of flight, caused by the pursuit of or dream of a subject which shimmers and sweeps me along but which can't and mustn't be taken, grasped, captured. It pants. This is what I love in Stendhal – the journals. The seat of the secret. It is there, there, here! The writing runs circles around it.

Staying with L'Ange *and* Jours de l'an(ge), *the expression of a difficulty, signaled, what's more, in the text: "This journey was having trouble getting started [. . .]. It was a journey which came from afar, from the back of the past at least. Mine or that of my ancestors. I can feel it in the heavy swell of the centuries"* (L'Ange au secret, *p. 10). Or again, among many other examples: "The author has almost finished [. . .]. The end is only a matter of a few lines, a decision. At that moment everything stops. The child cannot be born, doesn't want to be born"* (Jours de l'an, *p. 172).*

I see many things in this, such as the desire for an elsewhere, a passage, an impression perhaps confirmed in the text, and which would be linked with the "back of the past": "What I do in these final instants – for I feel that they are the final ones – is very difficult: I try to note the passage – I am in the act of passing. [. . .] And afterwards they'll say that you are obscure. Obscure? Obviously. How would the author not be: just before the revelation?" (ibid., p. 47). "We are painting the passage," Montaigne would say.

So I am guided, I let myself go along with this idea of a new transitional phase before you reach the shores of Or, Les lettres de mon père *in 1997 (but already one can notice this turning point toward the story in the History, the story of a family in that of the century, in* La Fiançée juive. *A transition in the history of the writing and in the work of memory?*

Well you are no doubt right, *although* I only become aware of this through your reading: one is *in the transition* unawares. These must be transitional periods, but the person in whom "the passage" occurs or is announced knows nothing, is merely a stage. Our whole life is like that, don't you think: blind tides move it on, then one looks back one reads oneself, one can write oneself also, but this is after the fact, it makes a story, but one was never at the commands of the story. It's strange. One is never one's own contemporary, one leaps ahead of oneself and one tags along. So today I am incapable of saying which book came before which other book, even if I see "families" and recall certain filiations. Hence *Or* which *necessitated Osnabrück.* Necessity is secretly written: *née cécité* [born blind], or: *naissent ces cités* [are born these cities].

In L'Ange au secret *again, you declare your admiration for and fear of people who write "with ax and knife." Kafka comes to mind. Mostly, this doesn't seem to be your case, except maybe in these books. What metaphor would you use to designate your books in their ensemble? Is the commonplace (however, if it is common, it is not private and so much the better) metaphor of water for the feminine in contradiction with your cry to fire: "Fire! Fire! Fire! Fire! No, this is not a cry of fear [. . .]. I write this under fire's dictation . . ." ("Write walk on fire,"* L'Ange au secret, *p. 223) and the frequent presence of crime ("We need the crime scene," "Our dead our assassins". . .)?*

What a question! It fells me with its acuity, and strikes me in my ignorance! That said I am for the sound and fury, for the brink of the gulf. But that's not it! Which metaphor? Yes, fire maybe. But if I am to believe my dreams, I *run* or I am kept from running, toward and against death. Always there's someone who is about to die (a stranger, someone close, me) and who *in extremis* doesn't. As for crime, I could almost say that it's my brother, my brother the crime, and since it's my brother, therefore it is half me, and as it is my brother I only think of dreading it running away from it in vain and failing to prevent it. My *inner* brother. My blood brother, Pierre, is rather my innocent.

In any case, there's crime, frequently and always by surprise, every inch of the way. You never stop killing and committing suicide. I kill you/me. The only "just" attitude: not to deny it.

Cuernava, July 26–Arcachon, August 3, 2002

There are many different roads between the two books of which we speak, Jours de l'An/-nge au secret, *and of course the ones before and after it. At what point is a book finished for you, or does it remain unfinished to be continued in the next one (like* Or/Osnabrück, *which are two faces of a same coin or medallion)? If it isn't "finished" (closed), this book you are writing, are its fluxes transmitted, do they circulate toward an elsewhere, its exterior?*

Superb, luminous question. But in order to answer, how much darkness I must grope through! Already this assemblage of the titles *Jours de l'An/ge au secret* is brilliant, it feels like an apocalypse, as if you had pierced my own night.

What do the two have in common (I who didn't know!): first, yes, night, the day of the night, the dense thickness of the secret, l'An/gst which takes me by the throat, always, like the hand of grief, at the idea of not being able to say, never to say, not be able to celebrate except in the catacombs, to feel (I

134

rejoice in it all the same) the connection or alliance between the gesture of writing to dig up and re-bury, in the very act of recovering, the interminable pursuit of the shimmering and ungraspable avowal.

This interminability is probably what causes "the end" of each book, the interruption from lack of breath, the avowal, the only possible avowal, of defeat: I can't do it; which is also the cause of the rhythm, the haste, for the final defeat is only consented to after repeated, feverish attacks, I turn back, I besiege, and I always hope. You never know. Maybe one New Year's Day – which I don't believe in – (and which perhaps I fear more than I desire) the secret will make an uncontrolled, fateful, and probably fatal irruption.

In these two texts, neither of whose affinity and confinity I had seen, the figures of the great Theater of writing are evoked, victims all of the same evil as me, the fate which consists in being witness to and so accomplice and hostage of the evil, the crime, of which we are composed, including as innocents, and which makes me think that wherever there is writing there is a threat of death or betrayal, in which the writing participates – it is part of the plot – which it palliates – which it would like to remedy, a wish at once vain and impious.

Probably, a hypothesis that you whisper to me, the structural in-sufferance of a text engenders the urgent call for help to its successor. However, the figures of these engenderings or pairings are not the same.

Hence *Or–Osnabrück* share very specific and largely accidental intercausalities. In this domain they definitely are a couple, the return of a marriage (my father my mother) not at all foreseen or planned at the outset. In writing *Or*, I had no other (H)/or/izon than *Or*. It was a battle against the couple my father and me, and a fight between my father-and-his-doubles and me, that wholly occupied me. The event that sparked it was in itself of a strength and a surprisingness such that it imposed itself as *coup de littérature* (like a *coup de théâtre*). That gave rise on my part to a non-literary, subjective, private resistance, I didn't want to raise the barrier between literature and life, I lived that as reciprocal intrusions. The-letters-of-my-father struck me like a bomb. However, bombs are literary events. When they fall they throw up sprays of story. None of that was expected. The postman of the "truth," my brother, totally unaware of what sort of "booby-trap letter" he was bringing me, and why on that particular day.

From *Or*, and probably in a fairly rapid latent manner, sprang the *obligation* for a sort of fairness or justice, an appeal – a judgment without appeal, something which had to come from the most ancient antiquity of my existence, and which draws the internal sides of my psyche, mother's side father's side, as Jacques Derrida showed in his text on me (*H.C. pour la vie, c'est à dire. . .*).

That the book's unfinishedness should open onto an elsewhere or exterior as you suppose is probably true. There is a remainder. If there was an analyst forceful and intimate enough to go and see, I imagine that one could bring to the light a sort of continuum life–work–life; and it is even likely that "my mother," the personage that she is for me in everyday life, would be transformed, distanced-brought close, haloed, by what I write or don't write about her, by her double status. (And not just her, but the others.)

On numerous occasions you've said that you only vaguely remembered a book that I was asking you about. You "forget" your books: is this (blackboard-like) erasure necessary in order to write again in the space, newly vacant, available, of the erased board?

The forgetting of my books goes back to the *forgetread* of which I've spoken (was this in *Or*? I forget) without which there'd be no more reading for me. I can read the books I love a hundred times and each time it's another book that turns up even if it's the same, as in love.

As for my own texts, it's the same movement in reverse: I no longer want to hear their voice. Also the idea of remembering them, clinging to them, or of quoting myself is disagreeable. (Same movement of forgetting and effacing for my personal history, events and people.) I don't look back. My amnesia is titanesque. And the people who remember or recall this or that scene or phrasing or situation petrify me. They seem like curators of dead things. Not that I forget the main ideas or important events. But I pick and choose (not on purpose), in the interest of what's to come, it must be like a computer, in effect I make space. For example for the theater, since at the moment I am writing for the theater, at the Théâtre du Soleil we dismantle the set, we knock the stage down, we start from zero. Me too. In the beginning, the desert. Ditto for the setting of the daily writing: no setting, the sky. No furniture. In a corner a painting by Frédéric-Yves, the only one, but it is writing. The original ignorance reconstituted. What makes spring come is the void.

Are the 1990s books, about which I'm questioning you now, more "present" than the earlier ones (is your memory of them still accessible, can it be mobilized) or are they erased as perfectly, as quickly as the older texts?

In my view they share more or less the same fate, no special treatment. In any case I affirm that the time of a work is not linear but circular or spherical, and all the little asters[37] or disasters are equidistant from the heart.

Of course, it would be possible *to analyze* analytically the

---

[37] *Astres* in French, meaning "stars."

power of such erasure, it must be ambivalent, a complicated machine in which life and death follow each other like seasons, something must die before the new growth. It is also an acceptance of the unacceptable, a detachment, the loss of the most dear, always life. Quick, I make haste to close the wounds. *But* there is also *in my life* the unforgettable never-to-be-forgotten, never over, never growing pale, and forever from the first day, and predating any vision or ascertainment, kept unaltered, intact, as if having been *before* the promised time, this is what most astonishes me, it's very rare, but it exists.

Cuernavaca-Arcachon, August 8–11, 2002

"Writing what turns up is risky, it's a kind of humility that can be a kind of pride like all humility, but one must run the risk," you write in L'Ange au secret *(p. 94). And a little further along: "My project was to tell the truth." Can the truth only be attained by the tricking of the unconscious which consists in "telling what turns up," hence letting the ungovernable text govern us?*

I sense I can only respond to this vast question humbly and inadequately. It would take a book, three essays. First a comment about "my project was to tell the truth." There, right away, me, the subject, split in two. Someone in me *wants* to tell the truth, desires, wishes, aspires, but *in* this same someone someone keeps watch without any illusions regarding the vanity of this desire, and aware that Truth is a pretty name for an illusion, which doesn't mean that one doesn't desire that which one calls *truth*. Besides for me "tell the truth" is defined in opposition to lying. It's an attempt not-to-lie, and especially to flush out a secret. I know this will never happen. So my desire is a widow and unconsoled.

So whatever there is of "truth" is found in the desire, the

shadow, the silhouette, the allusion. "What turns up" on the other hand is given. Is unauthorized, sent, an event. The risk is that *this* not be as fresh or marvelous as one imagines; one has perhaps said it already and better. At least the *turn up*, in itself, contains a dose of the unknown.

I allow myself to be led [*Je me laisse conduire*] (note the ambiguity of this expression!). I cultivate that which comes naturally, submission. As I dream. A frequent and fruitful process. A way to surrender. It liberates, relaxes, calms. I love to go to bed to dream (this happens to me during the day as well). I have the feeling I stop working, and trust myself. I have a great deal of confidence in this region from which visions, messages come. If I dared I would publish a collection of my dreams. For me they are enchanting. Magical thoughts, effortless. But what I write is a mixture of gnarled, extenuating effort, aiming for, seeking, and flowing from the other world, blessed, graceful.

The dreamt of book of dreams, Rêve je te dis, *was published after this interview, in September 2003.*

THE GRACE THE GALLOPING

Most, if not all, of your books – this is especially noticeable in those from the 1990s that we are exploring or rather galloping by (let's take Déluge, *from 1992, as a paradigm) – open with a cavalcade, shower, a rhythmical fulfillment and an elevation [*exaucement et exhaussement*], a plunge or an acceleration, a piece of pure rhythm, of happiness, elation, etc., in a clearly defined prosody: octo-, deca-, heptasyllables, alexandrines, with or without a caesura at the hemistich, etc. (Some examples among a hundred others: ". . . mon espace échauffé de lourdes chevauchées" ["my space in the heat of thundering rides"] (p. 12); ". . . ces bêtes nourries*

139

de chair aimée / qui allons à cheval / sans repos sans fatigue / dans la gueule du temps . . ." ["these beasts fed on loved flesh / who ride / without rest or fatigue / into time's jaws"] – my cuts.) *Only afterwards does "the story" begin, progressing more slowly, a tenacious seeking linked to a moment of the past, the present, and the scene of the writing. What for you are the modalities and protocols of a book's opening, and, not to limit ourselves to the idea of incipit, let's say: of the overture, in the musical sense, which introduces the themes? This idea of the beginning is not without its importance since it contributed the title of one of your first books* [Les Commencements], *and it is also present in the most recent,* Manhattan: Lettres de la préhistoire.

The entries, overtures, starts – this is a story in itself. I hold myself responsible: for more than once have these entries, antechambers, vestibules been pointed out to me, and not always with approval. Certain friends (Betrand Leclair, for example) have wondered if this is a defensive construction, a way of differing, brushing off, sizing up the reader (these are my words, I translate). Food for thought. So there you are: it occurs to me that I could or should shorten (by a head, hence) my text, strip it down, give faster access, etc. – make a strong gesture, perhaps this would be better. But I can't decide. I also feel the opposite necessity. This is, indeed, in the musical domain. Perhaps a means of transport. Physically I feel the need of a passage, a time of entry, as for an initiation, a bridge toward the other shore. A warning. All this, this period, this meander, wouldn't exist in the theater, where entry takes place in a single step and plays on abruptness.

I like metaphorical differing, spending time among the signs before the race. I have admiration – but also a sort of repulsion – for classical openings, expeditive, with a date, a situation, etc., which *abduct* the reader; but I am more riverine. I don't say it's good, better, worse, because I think such choices depend on libidinal structures, different paths to pleasure. I add that this is my poetic side, independent of genre, time of/on/language. It must be my bardic side. Something like a missing scene, probably musical, a moment of tuning up.

As for *Manhattan* and its opening chapter, it's like a cirque (in the mountains), it sketches a setting, it allows for taking in – *encaisser*[38] – (excuse the word, such a lovely one, all the same), for excavating and in-cavating, building a balcony from which to observe. And I must add that my books turn up also in this manner, by hidden leaps, racing backwards, fleeing from me; hence with their prehistory.

Similarly at the end of all your books, an all but invariable "pattern":[39] *shorter sentences in the denouement, a coming to rest. Does each book, beyond its intrinsic differences with all the others, follow, respond to a similar route or itinerary?*

You are referring to something – a "theme," a "presence" – that is increasingly close to me, haunting, which is this inner space inhabited, populated by the character that is the book itself. I write "a book" and this book lodges itself within me, a passerby, a guest, it exists in flesh and words; and I get to know this complex, composed but unique being, creature, I discover it as we go along. Its vital, animal part is very strong. Moreover it uses my body to make a body, members, for itself, to increase and divide itself into characters. As when I dream and people, at times complete strangers, populate me and I myself become a novel of a kind, in which I am myself a character who has heaps of adventures, *and* assault and battery.

There are always lots of animal, terrestrial, geographic bodies. And this is something that happens over and over

---

[38] *Encaisser* is rich in meaning, from "cashing" to "receiving a blow."
[39] In English in the original French text.

again in my texts without, in my view, becoming an artifice, of the comparative sort, but rather a simple inscription of the states of our psyche; our facility, often not well known or denied, for metamorphosis. We are tempestuous, full of changes. That's why I love what I see from my window, which doesn't seem in the least exterior to me, even if it's outside: huge stirring of the oak tree branches, a palm grove of winds, a flotilla of vegetable sailboats, and all that – swept, rained upon, flooded, lit up again – is not separate from my dreaming corporality. When I go galloping, well, it's that I am galloped. It's limitless, what's more, for I also sometimes accomplish deeds I am incapable of in reality but not in a dreamt representation, I can fly, swim through the air. And vice versa: I can also be the site of powerlessness and dreadful paralysis. I am the docile scribe of all these forms, I invent nothing, I note, I copy. And I take joy in them. For wherever language lives, whatever hurts also helps.

What you put your finger on in your question is the rhythm of these voyages. This rhythm is undoubtedly always part of the same scheme of things, since it is swept along by the race which starts and is in the end exhausted. I love Beethoven's symphonies like sisters. And yesterday I was listening to the songs of Richard Strauss, with extreme astonishment, because of how equally and interminably they proceed. It's spellbinding. But they make me feel how much I love precipitation, the precipice, the fall, the rapid diminishment. The book runs away with itself, to my great delight.

Strauss, Mahler, Gluck, German romanticism and expression-ism, as well as your love of Kleist, then Beethoven à jamais *(the symphonies, and no doubt the last quartets?) – there we have an elective but also selective affinity, which seems to come from afar. . . What is the role of music, this music, in your writing?*

142

My musics: they seem to me diverse, but perhaps they are the same or similar. I suspect myself of misappropriation, since in music I am ignorant, I am only a pleasure-seeker. The only musician in my family was my paternal grandmother, who played the piano – but this was long ago and elsewhere.

Music is within me and necessary, I write to music, to the rhythm, to its panting, and especially to its singing. Then sometimes something comes to me by chance, such or such a work, thus Britten's *Sumidagawa*, which moves me deeply, or Philip Glass's *Satyagraha*. This summer, 2002, Bartok's *Bluebeard* has bewitched me. When this happens I am (like everybody I guess) suddenly obsessed: I listen to the same work a hundred times, it's only one. That's why I think that basically there *is* only one, which comes back in different forms and colors but related. And at the bottom what or who is it? I have no idea. I imagine that it's the lost voice of my father, gone forever, forever, and which was lilting, jubilant and that I've never heard again. At one time I loved my mother's voice, a very plain alto. My father must have been a baritone. And as it turns out, I soprano. But I love altos – and countertenors, the deep pieces that are the most tender, I have a passion for certain mezzos which can-go-deep (like Marilyn Horne), these are broad spacious voices, in whose bottom a tomb is open (is not closed) and up at the top, the crown of a tree. These voices make me want to weep. I have written a lot about that; or weptwritten?

So to match these voices music that is voicelike, Mahler or Beethoven.

Beethoven: the 5th Symphony, in 1942, on my father's gramophone with a needle. It seemed to be the whole of music, music's essence. Even clawed and scratched.

But the quartets: I spent the whole summer of *Beethoven. . .* listening to them in all possible versions, certain sonatas also, but the quartets again again, in fact I could say they wrote the book (it's not completely true – but –). I've often thought that music is to me as fuel is to a motor, if humans have such a thing, it's the power, the *physis*, the joy of the pain. But I add that there are times when I write without music: for the theater we part company. There are already so many voices to listen to when one is writing a play, and curiously these are timbreless, ghostly, spiritual voices. For *pleasure*, verging on entertainment, I can also listen to a lot of Chopin or Schubert, a great great deal of Schumann. I set Monteverdi aside, for me he is close to writing, he is the tip. Curiously I've never adored Bach, I have always wondered what I lacked what ear. But doubtless, in adding Kleist to the inventory, you've hinted at an answer. I am "romantic" in the German way – which the Germans in my family have never been. To the point of tears [*Cela touche aux larmes*].

"Cela touche aux larmes" – there's a sentence that will be left hanging in the interpretation.

*

On the subject of punctuation (already touched upon): yours is completely idiosyncratic: dashes, white spaces, heterodoxical places to breathe, in and between sentences, parentheses which at times remain open, like held notes. An important element in creating a personal style is the personal and absolutely unique respiration, which is each writer's punctuation. Have you codified all that, can you speak about it or is it a matter of physiology, of your natural respiration?

Punctuation: no, I have not codified it: it follows me and I follow it [*elle me suit et je la suis*]. But it is absolute in its authority, it bothers me that people want me to correct it. I do sometimes add a few commas afterwards,[40] sensing the

---

[40] As the translator occasionally adds a comma or semi-colon when the

144

reader's need, but I find this absurd, obedient, false. There are sentences without full stops, nailing them down is needless repetition. But I have never been able to make myself heard on this vital extravagance, save by Derrida.

I can "speak about it," part of it does indeed come from the blood and the air's circulation, from the apnee of the heart's contraction, but another part is thinking thought refusal of the yoke and the need to allow amphibology to play to get close to thought at its inception, when it has not yet finished unfurling and has no full stops and above all no commas. Scholastic punctuation often strikes me as a multitude of little crutches, and why? It takes from the writing's flights [*Ça vole l'écriture*].

*

Do the dates that appear in the body of the text, a recent phenomenon (if I'm not mistaken, starting with Or, Les lettres de mon père*), correspond to a change of pace, rhythm, breath? There again, can you conceptualize this passage from a closed, timeless text to texts strewn with dates, at times like a journal? It's something that strikes me as becoming increasingly prominent (systematic in* Manhattan *and after).*

The dates, well, I'll have to go and take a closer look. But for starters: dates delight me, always, I don't take them literally but as a phantasm, as in this case, a wonderful and totally fictional punctuation of time, as a sign of humanity swimming in time, and attempting to stitch up the sea. I am not obsessive, dates for me are butterflies, they alight, they flit further along they have a vast magic and *secret* power for if I say 1930 or 1935 for each reader the origins unfold

---

English seems to require it in order to clarify phrasing that, in the English word order, is ambiguous, but not in a fruitful way.

different associations, a different kaleidoscope. They are like signals that sound, announcements that say: open your memory. The dates are also the pawns in chess, they play another game under the game I'm playing. But I never date them.

When they start to knock at the window of certains texts, it's because they are expected as characters. They have their effects, their drama. They are theatrical. It's like in a play: one has to say where one is, what time it is so the human characters can make their entry. When there are dates, a scene is being carved out of the text, fate starts to filter in. And then dates, I don't allow myself to entrust them with a referential value, they are almost always fictional, displaced, disguised. But they gallop, they accelerate what would be a slowing down of the story.

Manhattan: there the dates are to give a fragmented and crazy narration its apparent "proof" of reality.

(1) That "really" happened *one* time.

(2) It's in the past.

(3) This past remains present.

(4) There's an ongoing struggle between the will to report the event and the impossibility of doing so.

It's a human thing, a bolt of lightning, an atomic bomb, whose consequences endure, are not effaced, things continue, they continue beyond the duration of a human life, it *is* ongoing.

*

New York, September 2001–Arcachon, August 2002

You didn't completely agree when I told you the other day on the telephone that in reading Benjamin à Montaigne *for the first time I felt I was continuing the same book (the one that started with the dyptic* Or/Osnabrück, *two O's two "or"s, two "eaux" or perhaps*

146

two "os"?)[41] *It seems to me that from book to book, very differently no doubt, you are constructing your "big book" – your* À la recherche du temps perdu, *that you are pursuing the same "novel."*

Perhaps. Basically I have no idea. Things come along. I don't project. A book sprouts. Grows. No doubt it's a cousin? Or maybe one leans on the other? My impression: I stagger on, not seeing what's ahead (I don't have an idea or a blueprint). But the theme In search of lost time is not, in any case, lacking pertinence, except that I have no goal, still the Time theme is everywhere present, it is surely in my thoughts in its more threatening forms: no time, limited time (my mother's age), and so on.

And: the incredible richness of the times of time.

What orients me is rather what I can't say. I revolve around an absolute interdiction.

"I'm going to write to save that which must stay secret," you say in Beethoven à jamais.

God's returns

Rereading the July 2002 questions and answers – in particular those that focus on violent themes: water, axes, fire, crime – I said to myself, in a reproachful tone, that I am secretive – I stubbornly hide myself away – from what would constitute an unveiling. That perhaps all my writing has always been concealed (from me, from others) by a tendency

---

[41] The French text plays here on the long "o" sound of *eaux*, *os* ["water," "bone"] and the meaning of "*or*," gold.

toward secretness. That perhaps I might *one day respond* to this evasiveness, stop being secretive, face up to it, *deliver* [*livrer*] a few fragments if not the whole "Secret," face up to it, head-on, avow.

If I order myself to avow, what will I say, with as few detours as possible?

Perhaps this:

In the center of my life and my thought there is the shadow, the trace, the impression, or the illusion of a crime of which I might be the author. And more precisely: the enigma of the crime, the mystery of the idea of crime. This crime is not a crime. Seen by God and by me it's even the opposite of a crime, it is an innocent action, but very costly, very danger-ous. Seen by others it might be considered a crime. I can only compare this scene because of the extenuating cruelty of its ambivalence to the state of the soul (described by Kierkegaard in *Fear and Trembling* then revived and unfolded by Derrida in *Donner la Mort*) of Abraham, whose destiny is to be of two spheres, that of the absolute and that of the general or ethical. From the absolute viewpoint (God and no one else) Abraham is Justice and Innocence personified. From the general (soci-ety, law, morality) viewpoint he is an assassin, an infanticide, etc. I myself have always felt that, I've always had my soul in these two spheres, I've always been as innocent as I've been criminal and all the more the one as the other.

Since, like everyone else, I inhabit the sphere of the gen-eral, of the moral, I can only assume this radical division within myself and silently. I don't know how it began, this heartrending, rent, and yet allied, double stance, I don't know when it began, I see hints of it, first versions, first manifesta-tions early in my existence, at each death of someone close, of which I was guilty-innocent. But it is at the heart of my life-with-as-writing, at the heart of the writing of my life, that the instant I began to write/or/live, both together, the crime entered and has never ceased to haunt and inspire me. I am devoted to this event. Which has happened. Which remains nameless, addressless, appearanceless, guiltless, faultless for it exists only in Secret. It's one of the species of the Dream. When a Secret extends through time, it ends up being an inner land, a well of dreams, a second story which becomes main and immortal around a character of ordinary dimensions, let's say average-sized, but with extraordinary powers. It is the breath, the genius, the master (who can be feminine), the baby that gives life, and obligation, and that feeds the worst kinds of anguish, for when one writes one is always afraid to see it go away.

To return to Abraham, an uncommon personage, the ancestor of all tragedy, I have never understood or accepted in what one might call the Abrahamide or the Abramides, the play about Hagar and Ishmael. The Judeo-Christian world always spares itself the bother of a meditation around these unprecedented infamous – *if* one leaves them unexamined – events. True, Abraham had compassion for Hagar, and God assures him that he is going to take care of the woman and the first son, etc. One can gloss, justify on the level of the absolute as on that of the general. But I have always preferred to imagine that this episode of Genesis was perhaps a screen, a way of detecting the idiosyncracies, and of dissimulating another of Abraham's secrets, another inavowable division, for example, a fateful love for Hagar, that couldn't, that wouldn't have been able to subsist across the millennia except disguised as its opposite: hence a crime legitimized by God might cover a crime caused by God, etc. That's a little how I imagine intimate human relations, as always relegated to the deserts, to the underground, criss-crossed, fearful and wonderful, but bearing a threat of death. Fairy tales do this too: so often life depends upon a word that mustn't be said; or that shouldn't have been said; or that ought to have been said. . .

HÉLÈNE CIXOUS:
SELECT BIBLIOGRAPHY

1. In English

The Exile of James Joyce. Translated by Sally A. J. Purcell. New York: David Lewis–London: John Calder, 1976.

Portrait of Dora. Translated by Anita Barrows. *Gambit International Theater Review* 8, no. 30 (1977): 27–67. Reprinted in *Benmussa Directs*. Playscript 91. London: John Calder–Dallas: Riverrun (1979): 27–73.

Vivre l'orange/To Live the Orange (bilingual French/English). Translated by Ann Liddle and Sarah Cornell. Paris: Des femmes–Antoinette Fouque, 1979.

Angst. Translated by Jo Levy. London: John Calder–New York: Riverrun, 1985.

The Conquest of the School at Madhubaï. Translated by Deborah W. Carpenter. *Women and Performance* 3, Special Feature (1986): 59–95.

Inside. Translated by Carol Barko. New York: Schocken Books, 1986.

The Newly Born Woman. Translated by Betsy Wing. Minneapolis: University of Minnesota Press–Manchester: Manchester University Press, 1986 (*with Catherine Clément*).

Reading with Clarice Lispector. Translated by Verena Andermatt Conley. Minneapolis: University of Minnesota Press–London: Harvester Wheatsheaf, 1990.

The Book of Promethea. Translated by Betsy Wing. Lincoln: University of Nebraska Press, 1991.

"Coming to Writing" and Other Essays. Edited by Deborah Jenson. Translated by Sarah Cornell, Deborah Jenson, Ann Liddle, and Susan Sellers. Cambridge, MA: Harvard University Press, 1991.

The Name of Oedipus. In *Plays by French and Francophone Women: A Critical Anthology*. Edited and translated by Christiane Makward and Judith G. Miller. Ann Arbor: University of Michigan Press, 1991.

Readings: The Poetics of Blanchot, Joyce, Kafka, Kleist, Lispector, and Tsvetayeva. Edited and translated by Verena A. Conley. Minneapolis: University of Minnesota Press–London: Harvester Wheatsheaf, 1992.

Three Steps on the Ladder of Writing. Translated by Sarah Cornell and Susan Sellers. New York: Columbia University Press, 1993.

The Hélène Cixous Reader. Edited and translated by Susan Sellers. London–New York: Routledge, 1994.

Manna, for the Mandelstams for the Mandelas. Translated by Catherine A. F. MacGillivray. Minneapolis: University of Minnesota Press, 1994.

The Terrible but Unfinished Story of Norodom Sihanouk, King of Cambodia. Translated by Juliet Flower MacCannell, Judith Pike, and Lollie Groth. Lincoln: University of Nebraska Press, 1994.

Bloom. Dublin: Kingstown Press, 1996.

Rootprints: Memory and Life Writing. Translated by Eric Prenowitz. London–New York: Routledge, 1997 (*with Mireille Calle-Gruber*).

First Days of the Year. Translated by Catherine A. F. MacGillivray. Minneapolis: University of Minnesota Press, 1998.

Stigmata. Escaping Texts. London–New York: Routledge, 1998.

The Third Body. Translated by Keith Cohen. Evanston, IL: Hydra Books–Northwestern University Press, 1999.

Veils. Translated by Geoffrey Bennington. Stanford: Stanford University Press, 2001 (*with Jacques Derrida*).

Portrait of Jacques Derrida as a Young Jewish Saint. Translated by Beverley Bie Brahic. New York: Columbia University Press, 2003.

Selected Plays. Edited by Eric Prenowitz. London: Routledge, 2003.

The Writing Notebooks. Edited and translated by Susan Sellers. New York: Continuum, 2004.

Dream I Tell You. Translated by Beverley Bie Brahic. New York: Columbia University Press, 2006.

Ex-cities. Edited by Aaron Levy and Jean-Michel Rabaté. Philadelphia: Slought Books, 2006.

Reveries of the Wild Woman. Primal Scenes. Translated by Beverley Bie Brahic. Evanston, IL: Northwestern University Press, 2006.

Insister of Jacques Derrida. Translated by Peggy Kamuf. Edinburgh: Edinburgh University Press, 2007.

Love Itself in the Letter Box. Translated by Peggy Kamuf. Cambridge: Polity Press, 2008.

White Ink: Interviews on Sex, Text, and Politics. Edited by Susan Sellers. New York: Columbia University Press, 2008.

2. In French

Le Prénom de Dieu. Paris: Grasset, 1967. Reprinted in 1985.

L'Exil de James Joyce ou l'art du remplacement. Paris: Grasset, 1968.

Dedans. Paris: Grasset, 1969. Reprinted by Des femmes–Antoinette Fouque, 1986.

Les Commencements. Paris: Grasset, 1970. Reprinted by Des femmes–Antoinette Fouque, 1999.

Le Troisième Corps. Paris: Grasset, 1970. Reprinted by Des femmes–Antoinette Fouque, 1999.

Un vrai jardin. Paris: L'Herne, 1971. Reprinted by Des femmes–Antoinette Fouque, 1998.

Neutre. Paris: Grasset, 1972. Reprinted by Des femmes–Antoinette Fouque, 1998.

La Pupille. Paris: *Cahiers Renaud-Barrault* 78, 1972.

Portrait du soleil. Paris: Denoël, 1973. Reprinted by Des femmes–Antoinette Fouque, 1999.

Tombe. Paris: Seuil, 1973. Reprinted in 2008.

Prénoms de personne. Paris: Seuil, 1974.

La Jeune Née. Paris: Christian Bourgois, 1975 (*with Catherine Clément*).

Un K. incompréhensible: Pierre Goldman. Paris: Christian Bourgois, 1975.

Révolutions pour plus d'un Faust. Paris: Seuil, 1975.

Souffles. Paris: Des femmes–Antoinette Fouque, 1975. Reprinted in 1998.

La. Paris: Gallimard, 1976. Reprinted by Des femmes–Antoinette Fouque, 1979.

Partie. Paris: Des femmes–Antoinette Fouque, 1976. Reprinted in 1998.

Portrait de Dora. Paris: Des femmes–Antoinette Fouque, 1976. Reprinted in *Théâtre.* Paris: Des femmes–Antoinette Fouque, 1986.

La Venue à l'écriture. Paris: U.G.E., 1976 (*with Madeleine Gagnon and Annie Leclerc*).

Angst. Paris: Des femmes–Antoinette Fouque, 1977. Reprinted in 1998.

Préparatifs de noces au-delà de l'abîme. Paris: Des femmes–Antoinette Fouque, 1978.

Le Nom d'Œdipe Chant du corps interdit. Paris: Des femmes–Antoinette Fouque, 1978.

Ananké. Paris: Des femmes–Antoinette Fouque, 1979.

Vivre l'orange. Paris: Des femmes–Antoinette Fouque, 1979.

Illa. Paris: Des femmes–Antoinette Fouque, 1980.

With ou l'Art de l'innocence. Paris: Des femmes–Antoinette Fouque, 1981.

Limonade tout était si infini. Paris: Des femmes–Antoinette Fouque, 1982.

Le Livre de Prométhéa. Paris: Gallimard, 1983.

La Prise de l'école de Madhubaï. Paris: *Avant-Scène–Théâtre* 475, 1984. Reprinted in *Théâtre*. Paris: Des femmes–Antoinette Fouque, 1986.

L'Histoire terrible mais inachevée de Norodom Sihanouk, roi du Cambodge. Paris: Théâtre du Soleil, 1985.

La Bataille d'Arcachon. Québec: Trois, 1986.

Entre l'écriture. Paris: Des femmes–Antoinette Fouque, 1986.

L'Indiade, ou l'Inde de leurs rêves, et quelques écrits sur le théâtre. Paris: Théâtre du Soleil, 1987.

Manne aux Mandelstams aux Mandelas. Paris: Des femmes–Antoinette Fouque, 1988.

L'Heure de Clarice Lispector. Paris: Des femmes–Antoinette Fouque, 1989.

Jours de l'an. Paris: Des femmes–Antoinette Fouque, 1990.

Karine Saporta. Paris: Armand Colin, 1990 (*with Daniel Dobbels and Bérénice Reynaud*).

L'Ange au secret. Paris: Des femmes–Antoinette Fouque, 1991.

On ne part pas, on ne revient pas. Paris: Des femmes–Antoinette Fouque, 1991.

Déluge. Paris: Des femmes–Antoinette Fouque, 1992.

Beethoven à jamais ou l'existence de Dieu. Paris: Des femmes–Antoinette Fouque, 1993.

L'Histoire (qu'on ne connaîtra jamais). Paris: Des femmes–Antoinette Fouque, 1994.

Photos de racines. Paris: Des femmes–Antoinette Fouque, 1994 (*with Mireille Calle-Gruber*).

La Fiancée juive – de la tentation. Paris: Des femmes–Antoinette Fouque, 1995.

La Ville parjure ou le réveil des Érinyes. Paris: Théâtre du Soleil, 1995.

Messie. Paris: Des femmes–Antoinette Fouque, 1996.

Or, Les lettres de mon père. Paris: Des femmes–Antoinette Fouque, 1997.

Voiles. Paris: Galilée, 1998 (*with Jacques Derrida*).

Osnabrück. Paris: Des femmes–Antoinette Fouque, 1999.

Tambours sur la digue. Paris: Théâtre du Soleil, 1999.

Hélène Cixous, Croisées d'une oeuvre (Actes du colloque de Cerisy 1998). Edited by Mireille-Calle Gruber. Paris: Gallimard, 2000.

Le Jour où je n'étais pas là. Paris: Galilée, 2000.

Les Rêveries de la femme sauvage: Scènes primitives. Paris: Galilée, 2000.

Benjamin à Montaigne: Il ne faut pas le dire. Paris: Galilée, 2001.

Portrait de Jacques Derrida en jeune saint juif. Paris: Galilée, 2001.

Rouen, la trentième nuit de mai '31. Paris: Galilée, 2001.

Manhattan: Lettres de la préhistoire. Paris: Galilée, 2002.

Rêve je te dis. Paris: Galilée, 2003.